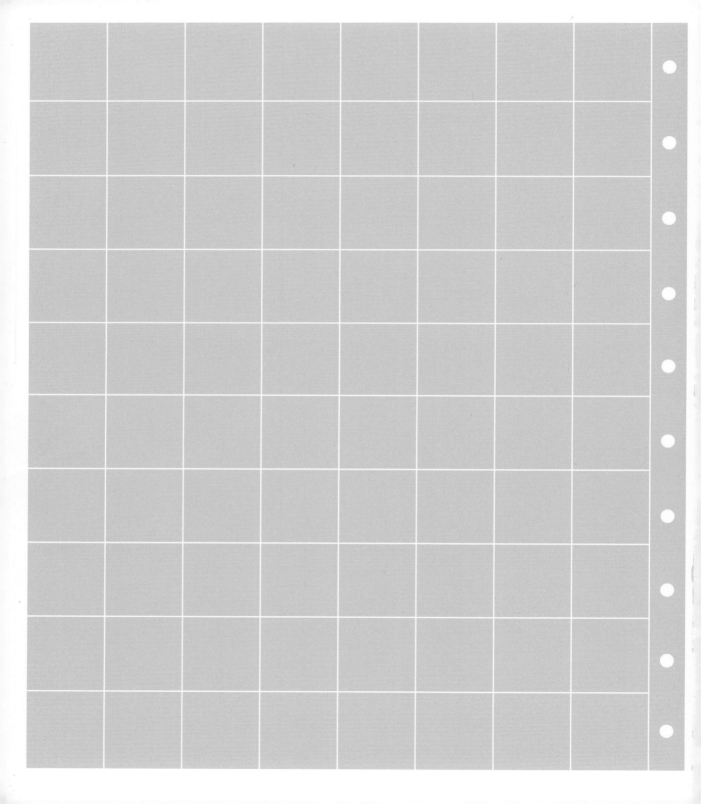

CARE PACKAGES
Michelle Mackintosh

CARE PACKAGE

noun 1. Also, CARE package.
a package containing food,
clothing, or other items sent
as necessities to the needy.

2. a gift of treats to relatives
or friends, especially of items
not readily available to them.

For my
dear Steve

CARE PACKAGES
Michelle Mackintosh

hardie grant books

Contents

Introduction

Discover the pleasure, charm and history of the humble care package. **65**

THIS WAY UP

Introduction

GREETINGS

and salutations

In today's busy world, it can be hard to find the time to stop, think and act when we know someone dear to us is struggling or has wonderful news. Everyone needs to be cared for at some point in their lives: not just when things are tough, but also in times of celebration and joy. These things are very important to me - and I hope they are to you, too! A care package for a loved one can be something grand or something so small you may not even think of it as a care package at all. Your gesture could make someone's day and, most importantly, the person in question will know you are thinking of him or her. After all, isn't that everything a care package could ever hope to be?

When I was two years old, I experienced my first care package. My older sister was to be flower girl at a wedding that I was too young to attend. I was sent to my grandmother's to be cared for and was not particularly happy about missing out. (Yes, I have an extremely good memory!) My grandmother was all prepared when I arrived. She had crocheted me a small bag filled with farm animals. She had also baked tiny savouries and cakes for us to feast on. To this day, it's one of my most cherished memories. She thought about what I would like and set about making an afternoon and evening that I would love. If you asked my grandmother if she thought she had given me a care package, she probably would have said no. But really, there is no 'box' to confine what a care package should be!

In times of happiness, sorrow or even everyday life, the act of stopping, thinking and acting is what is important. You can make things for loved ones, purchase items you know they will adore, take them somewhere special, or provide comfort, support and a listening ear. All of the above qualify as care packages, as could many more acts of kindness.

I'm lucky to have wonderful friends and family around me. The few times in my life where difficult things have happened to me, I've received the most wonderful care packages. When my father was very sick, I lived in the hospital for two weeks. My best friend Melinda came to the hospital with magazines, and she told me that when I was finished she would swap them over and bring more. She became my lending library,

and I knew she would be back with a refresh whenever I needed.

Years later I was in a car accident, and I received so many wonderful care packages. Before the accident, I would go and buy a special dinner after my husband's radio show on Fridays, but as I couldn't drive for nine months, my friends May and Olivia took over the task so our favourite meal was still provided for. My friends Jane and Will would bring me my favourite sandwich to the hospital and Jane and I would spend hours on the phone. Mum would buy my favourite tofu dishes and bring them in. Pacquita held my hand. Dawn and Ingrid were just 'around'. Any time I needed anything – help, comfort, a talk, a lift – they were there. Trisha, Rachel, and Mr T provided wonderful ongoing support. Andrew helped me in so many ways. And Melinda and Graham sent me the most thoughtful packages all the way from New York.

I am lucky to have the ultimate care package in my husband Steve. He has made me mix tapes for stressful work environments, put together a cosy pack after the accident, and is basically my human care package every day of the year. I am also lucky to have a furry stress relief care package in the form of my beautiful cat Bronte.

I love to make care packages for friends, and I hope that through these small offerings the people around me know how much I love and care for them.

I hope that you find some inspiration in these pages and that, if they aren't already, care packages become as important to you as they are to me.

two pounds of
margarine or
one pound of lard

one CRU (black)
water bottle

one pound of
raisins

one pound of steak
and kidneys,
eight ounces of
liver loaf, eight
ounces of corned beef

one pound of
beef in broth

two pounds of
sugar

one pound of
fruit preserves

CRU sunglasses

one pound of
honey

one pound of
chocolate

two pounds of
whole-milk powder

one Bible
and journal
one KGP booklet

twelve ounces of
luncheon loaf
(like Spam)

eight ounces of
egg powder

eight ounces of
bacon

two pounds of
coffee

A brief history of the CARE package

While care packages get their name from the humanitarian organisation Cooperative for Assistance and Relief Everywhere (CARE for short), which began distributing parcels of food and supplies in Europe following World War II, people have been sending packages of provisions to others as long as there has been a way.

During World War I, various charities and women's groups were set up all over the world to make care and comfort packages to send to soldiers. The parcels contained items that were useful, thoughtful, delicious or inspirational, and many inclusions were luxuries in wartime: tobacco, sweet biscuits, condensed milk and chocolate. Journals, books and bibles were also popular additions. Many women's magazines at the time contained knitting and sewing patterns for practical garments like socks, beanies and balaclavas. Thousands of women got involved and made precious treats and treasures for servicemen whom they would most likely never meet and who would perhaps never make it home.

This tradition was carried on throughout all of the conflicts of the twentieth and twenty-first centuries. As technology advanced, so did communication – and the contents of these parcels. Bulky wirelesses were replaced with tapes, CDs and now mp3 players and USB sticks, making music portable. Soldiers can now email and Skype. But even though technology has moved forward, the humble care package is still very much needed. Handwritten letters, video messages, homemade treats, photographs: all of these personal items help to keep your dearest's spirits up while reminding them of the people that love them at home.

Care packages aren't exclusively for soldiers, of course. Today, many members of our society receive and rely on them. Wonderful charities raise money to make and send parcels to the sick, elderly, marginalised and most needy in our communities. Individuals, families and friendship groups make care packages for friends, loved ones and strangers alike, not only for support during hard times but also in celebration or thanks. The care package has changed, adapted and found its way into popular culture.

Many of the items included in original wartime care packages would still be welcome additions to a parcel sent today: chocolate, dried fruit and nuts, honey, coffee and journals are compact little luxuries perfect for anyone in need of a little TLC. Of course, a modern care package is more likely to take into consideration a person's allergies or dietary requirements, and perhaps the questionable tinned meat of days gone by wouldn't go down quite so well. These days a surprise delivery of offal and spam would seem more like a don't-care package!

Over the years I have been the recipient of many wonderful care packages. And when I've made parcels, the act of helping someone else has helped me. In a time of crisis, when I'm unable to change the situation at hand, doing and making allows me to feel useful, like I can make a small contribution or help in some sort of tiny way. And it is this feeling, I believe, that is at the heart of the care package's enduring popularity.

What makes a great care package?

something thoughtful

something fun

something unexpected

something personal

something indulgent

You'll know best what's appropriate for your parcel: if you don't know the recipient, you can leave out something personal; if it's a package for a grieving friend, you may choose to omit something fun, but include something unexpected; and if it's a true love package, you'll include all of the above and more.

But what truly makes a great care package is the time you have taken to think about the recipient and make them something that is not only from the bottom of your heart; but also reflects who they are. If your loved one is into music, for instance, your package could be tied together with graphic flourishes from their favourite era (I love the '60s and '90s!); if they have a passion for a particular sport, you could decorate it in their team colours. It really is the thought that counts! So have fun, pretty something up and send your parcel off into the world. Giving can be just as fun (or even better) than receiving.

The human CARE package

For some situations, a prettily wrapped parcel is not appropriate or not enough. Sometimes, what your loved one really needs is time, company or a shoulder to cry on - or perhaps all of the above.

Oscar Wilde once wrote that 'to expect the unexpected shows a thoroughly modern intellect'. As a human care package, you need to be ready to listen for signals and adapt to the emotions at hand. Expect anything, bring everything, visit your friend and brighten their day.

1/ THE LISTENER

Your loved one may need to talk. If you sense this, shelve your witty stories and anecdotes for another day and make the effort to really listen. If there is a pause in the conversation, you might like to gently share your thoughts on some of the subjects raised – but refrain from giving advice unless it's directly asked for. It's important you turn your phone off, make proper eye contact and hold the connection. If something difficult is going on, you may be the only person your loved one is taking into their confidence.

2/ THE NEWS BRINGER AND THE WIT

If someone you love is in hospital or away from home, news from the outside world or a familiar place can provide welcome relief. Again, your antennae will need to be up and you will need to assess whether talking is the way to go. Before visiting your friend, perhaps read up on any topics you know they love. Bring in some newspaper clippings or print out a story you can discuss together. Speak of their favourite topics and people. Have a few funny stories up your sleeve, if you know they need cheering up. If your friend is unwell, talk of things you have done or enjoyed together, the things that connect you, the things you've both lived through. Whatever you discuss, put a little bit of thought into it before you enter the room. Your friend is going through something. How can you make his or her day brighter?

3/ THE MASSEUR

My mother has worked as a volunteer at a hospital for more than fifteen years, offering hand massages to patients. She doesn't ask questions; she's not a doctor or nurse; she's simply there to give someone a little bit of pampering. This is an option best reserved for your very nearest and dearest. You'll have to gauge whether a hand, foot or shoulder massage is appropriate, and if it is, whether any talking is required. For the right person, massage can be relaxing. It's also a way for you both to feel connected. If this is something your loved one enjoys, perhaps next time you can bring along some essential oils or a lovely hand cream, or you may be inspired to create a mini massage-themed care package.

Giving back to the community

For those of us who don't live in close-knit communities, the idea of gifting something to a stranger or even an acquaintance can seem a little daunting. But care packages need not be reserved for your nearest and dearest only - in fact, giving back to the community has long been part of the care package tradition. Thoughtfully prepared parcels full of useful items can sometimes mean more than the monetary gifts we often fall back on when we want to give back to the community.

include fruit or vegetables grown in your garden

homemade muesli (page 98), homemade roasted tomato sauce (page 102)

sweet treats can be a welcome addition

herbs or edible plants are perfect additions

Making a care package for someone special in your community who, for one reason or another, has made a difference in your life or the lives of your friends and family members is a lovely thing to do. The person may be a nurse or doctor who has cared for you, or perhaps a friend's family that has been kind to you. It may be your favourite teacher or sports coach, a long-time babysitter, or an elderly person, neighbour or beloved member of your community who you know is going through a hard time.

If you are moved or affected by someone's selfless behaviour, why not do something nice in return? The gesture doesn't need to be huge or expensive; it's all about the sentiment. Why not get a group of friends together and spend a Sunday afternoon making a special package? You could even organise an activity day with school friends, sporting team members or any group of people who have been touched by the individual's generosity.

ANONYMOUS PARCELS

For someone in a tough spot financially or otherwise, it can be difficult to accept help when offered. People are proud, and no one wants to feel pitied. But everyone needs a hand now and then whether they like to admit it or not. Carers, single parents and families affected by job loss or illness could all do with a little TLC.

A practical package is a wonderful surprise for someone in a stressful situation, and delivering it anonymously means that the recipient doesn't feel embarrassment or an obligation to reciprocate. Your care package is for the recipient to do with as he or she wishes.

Perhaps you know of a family struggling at Christmas, Hanukkah, Eid, Easter or Thanksgiving? A special food parcel could be a wonderful gesture. Perhaps it's school holidays and you know a single parent whose family could benefit from some treats – perhaps some movie vouchers or a fun board game?

The recipient of an anonymous care package doesn't necessarily need to be in financial strife or going through a tough time, either. Military personnel or aid workers away from their home comforts are great people to send an anonymous care package to. Your favourite charity or your country's armed forces will be able to provide information on how to send a package to their members overseas.

There are also plenty of local good causes to gift anonymous packages to, like your local animal shelter or council literacy program. You could give a donation of pens and paper to an after-school group or handmade soft toys to a children's hospital, or put together an afternoon tea package for your local homeless shelter. There are endless ways to use your creativity to help and to make a difference – even if your contribution is small and simple.

A FEW TIPS ON GIVING ANONYMOUS CARE PACKAGES

Don't fancy things up too much
Present your package simply and beautifully. Make sure you attach a large tag with the recipient's name, or else they may think the parcel is not for them.

Keep the contents practical
Include nicer versions of everyday items – things that may be too much of a stretch for a budgeted supermarket shop.

Add an element of fun or warmth
For example, if it's for Christmas, include some Christmas novelty socks or perhaps a handmade decoration.

Give a completely handmade care package if you're crafty or talented in the kitchen.
Sweets, baked goods, preserves, knitting, crochet, hand-sewn items, fruit and vegetables from your garden: these things are both practical and show that you are thinking of the recipient.

Getting it there

Before you buy a box, tin, jar or vintage suitcase, or think about making your package out of paper or fabric, you'll need to decide on the delivery method that suits your project and recipient best, as this will affect how large your parcel is and what you include in it.

BY POST

A trip to your local post office may be in order before you get started, so you can get an idea of the cost of sending your parcel by post; otherwise, most postal services' websites provide postage calculators. Remember, both size and weight count when it comes to cost! If you'd rather be safe than sorry, your postal service may offer flat-fee satchels or boxes.

You will be able to choose from a number of delivery speed options, with domestic regular post (roughly 2–8 days) being the cheapest and international express (1–2 days) being the most expensive. Being clever about what you include in a parcel (avoiding anything perishable, for instance) will help you save money.

If you want your parcel to arrive in time for a birthday, religious holiday or anniversary, always assume postage will take the maximum amount of time estimated (if not longer), and keep in mind delays caused by weekends and public holidays.

Make sure your parcel doesn't contain anything that could break and spoil the rest of its contents (and if you must send something fragile, make sure it is very, very well protected), and definitely do not send anything that is illegal or contraband. For the sake of your hard work and your recipient, please buy a padded bag, or fill your box with lots of packing material so your items don't move or break.

Most importantly, address your parcel clearly and double-check it before you send it. Always include your return address, in case something goes wrong.

BY COURIER

Generally more expensive than using the postal service, but usually faster and more reliable, using a courier is a good choice if you have edible goods in your parcel or if you need it delivered in a rush. Depending on which courier you use, price may be governed by standard box sizes or by weight. Do your research, find the best company for you and stick to their specifications. You may not be able to decorate the outside of the parcel with this option, so make sure everything inside it is nicely presented.

BY BICYCLE

You'll need to make sure your care package can fit into your bicycle's basket, parcel rack or pannier, and is not so heavy that it makes your ride difficult. To keep things light, you may choose to become a human care package (page 14) to go along with your parcel. Delivery by bicycle is a great way to get some exercise and enjoy neighbourhood life. So decorate up a storm, gather up some freshly baked goods, champagne, and a mix tape to listen to together, and go local!

BY FOOT OR BY CAR

The sky is the limit here: your parcel can be anything your imagination wishes! Food can be out-of-the-oven fresh; plants, flowers and fragile items are options; and you can go to town with balloons, streamers and decorations. If your loved one is home, why not leave the package on their doorstep and reveal the surprise with a cryptic text message? Or, if they have a secluded front garden and the parcel is small, you could leave it there for them to discover (just keep an eye on the weather!). If face-to-face contact is more your style, knock on the door and serenade your loved one while delivering the package, or if you know the recipient is going through a tough time, drop over with the package and hopefully you'll be invited in for a cup of tea and a chat.

Sizing things up

Here are some of the best items to include in small, medium and large packages. Small packages can usually be sent by post, although the weight of your parcel my determine the cost so please check with your post office before sending. Medium and large packages can be delivered on foot or by bicycle, public transport, courier or car.

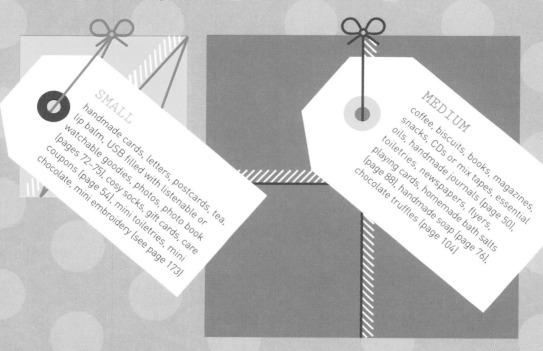

SMALL

handmade cards, letters, postcards, tea, lip balm, USB filled with listenable or watchable goodies, photos, photo book (pages 72–75), cosy socks, gift cards, care coupons (page 54), mini toiletries, mini chocolate, mini embroidery (see page 173)

MEDIUM

coffee, biscuits, books, magazines, snacks, CDs or mix tapes, essential oils, handmade journals (page 50), toiletries, newspapers, flyers, playing cards, homemade bath salts (page 88), handmade soap (page 76), chocolate truffles (page 104)

Choose your box size first

LARGE
cake or slice, champagne, wine, drinks, books, full-sized toiletries, magazines, fragile items, clothing, board games, picture frames

flammable goods

military items

live plants

live animals and
insects,
animal carcasses

aerosols

controlled drugs
and narcotics

dry ice

fresh fruit and
vegetables

extreme
pornography

cigarettes and
tobacco

matches

magnetised
materials

Things you may
not realise you
shouldn't send

batteries

money, cash,
cheques and some
lottery tickets

alcohol (subject
to local
guidelines)

perfumes containing
alcohol, nail
polish and remover

Postal faux pas

If you choose to, or need to, mail your care package, use your common sense and don't send anything illegal, dangerous or offensive. If you're sending something overseas, remember that what may be legal or appropriate in your country may not be in another.

It may seem obvious that it is against the law in most countries to send firearms by regular post, but did you know that mailing nail polish is a no-no? Opposite is a list of items that generally cannot be (or aren't recommended to be) sent through your postal service, keeping in mind there may be some variations from country to country. Fortunately, many of the items listed are not the kind of thing anyone would send if they were being caring or considerate. Having said that, there are a few items listed that I did not know were considered non-mailable goods.

When in doubt, check your postal or courier service's rules online or talk to your postmaster before you start to pack your parcel.

ROGUE ITEMS

Think before you pack your beloved a care package and send it via the post.

My friend Rihana was once sent a package full of books that also contained a bottle of wine. Of course, the bottle of wine broke and the books were ruined.

Even if your items are considered safe to send, make sure you individually package items that are delicate or breakable. If you're sending long-life food, pack it in a way that prevents it from being squashed or crumbled. Separate food from non-food items. You don't want your beautifully hand-knitted socks to smell like shortbread or fruitcake, do you? (Or perhaps you do.)

Thoughtfully packing a care package destined for the post can be a fun exercise. Make sure you're armed with bubble wrap, tissue paper, wax paper and shredded paper (or packing peanuts). And just because everything is securely protected and padded doesn't mean you can't pretty it up afterwards. Happy packing!

Cross-cultural gift giving

With the internet and international travel enabling us to connect with people all around the world, it's important to keep cultural differences in mind when putting together a care package for a friend, colleague or stranger who comes from a different country. While most reasonable people would forgive a simple faux pas (after all, it's the thought that counts), a little research can save you from embarrassment! Certain flowers, numbers or colours can carry connotations of bad luck or death. Red roses are universally known as the lover's bouquet. Additionally, in most cultures, an extravagant gift is seen as unusual.

ITEMS ASSOCIATED WITH FUNERALS AND DEATH

Japan
white flowers, chrysanthemums
gifts wrapped in white paper
white and black or white and yellow wrapping
(white and red wrapping is OK)

UK, Sweden
white lilies, chrysanthemums

Canada
white lilies

China
clocks
towels
white flowers, yellow chrysanthemums
white or black wrapping

Hong Kong
white or blue wrapping

Russia
yellow flowers
an even number of flowers

Mexico
red, purple or yellow flowers, marigolds

Morocco
anything pink, violet and yellow

Chile
purple or black flowers or wrapping

Norway
lilies, carnations, white flowers
even numbers of flowers or wreaths

Poland
red or white flowers, especially carnations
and lilies, yellow chrysanthemums

Spain
dahlias, chrysanthemums, white lilies

Malaysia
white wrapping (green or red are the safest choices)

India
frangipanis
black and white wrapping

ITEMS ASSOCIATED WITH ENDING FRIENDSHIPS OR RELATIONSHIPS

Switzerland, Germany, South America
knives

Middle East
handkerchiefs

China
handkerchiefs
umbrellas
scissors
knives
shoes

ITEMS ASSOCIATED WITH ROMANCE

Germany, Canada, the United Kingdom and
most western countries
red roses

Sweden
red roses, orchids

NUMBERS ASSOCIATED WITH BAD
LUCK

Japan
four, nine, thirteen

Korea
four

China
thirteen, any number ending with four

Peru
thirteen

Spain
flowers in odd numbers

India
items in multiples of three

ITEMS CONSIDERED RUDE OR
DISRESPECTFUL

France
a gift of wine brought to a party is seen as rude,
as the host should choose the vintage

Argentina
a woman should not give a gift to a male
colleague
a gift of wine is considered too common

Muslim countries
pork
alcohol
art or photographs featuring nudity
anything too personal, such as underwear
gifts with images of dogs, toy dogs

Mexico
red flowers are believed to cast spells
anything silver

China
flowers are only ever given to the sick or at
funerals
straw sandals
a green hat implies the recipient is a coward

India
leather products

Bangladesh
a gift of money, unless it is for a wedding

APPROPRIATE GIFTS AND
GIFTS ASSOCIATED WITH LUCK

China
anything red
wine is seen as a toast to the recipient's health
peaches are seen as gift of longevity
the number six is associated with good luck
the number eight is associated with prosperity

Israel and the Jewish religion
the number 126

LUCKY GIFTS AND SYMBOLS FOR
NEWLYWEDS

China
dates, peanuts, longans and lotus seeds, all
given together (this combination of ingredients
in Chinese translates as 'will get a baby soon')
money in a red envelope (at least sixty dollars,
but avoid the unlucky numbers listed above)

Scotland
a sprig of white heather

Italy
anything green is considered good luck

Russia
alcohol and wine signify celebration

Israel and the Jewish religion
a monetary gift in a multiple of eighteen

The Hindu religion
money with a value ending in one, in a
handmade gift envelope

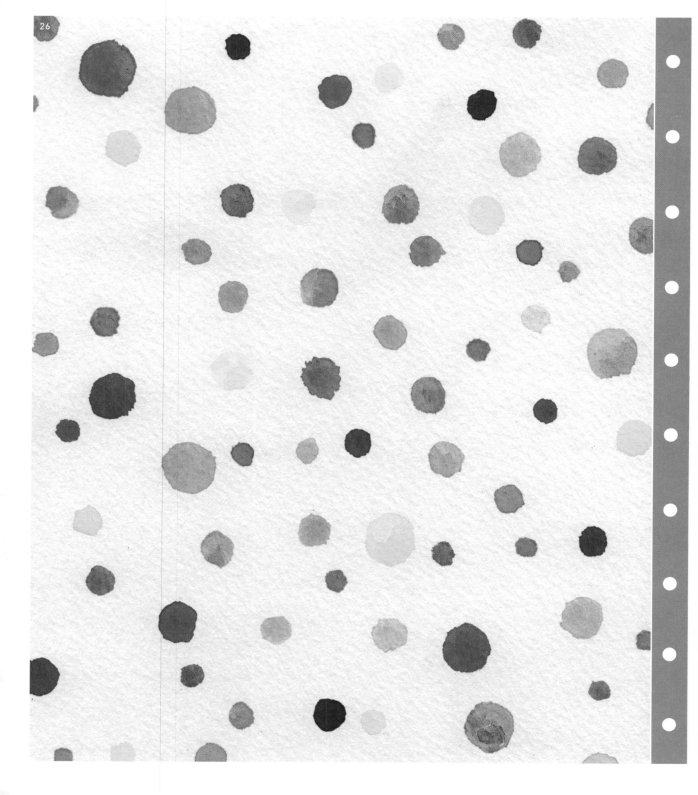

That's what I consider true generosity. You give your all, and yet you always feel as if it costs you nothing.

Simone de Beauvoir

You can make, personalise and send a care package for just about any reason. Be as simple or as over-the-top as you want – add humour, a surprise or a signature handmade flourish – so long as your creativity appropriately reflects the occasion and the recipient's personality. Something loud and outlandish sent to a grieving colleague, for instance, might send a message of insensitivity, rather than condolences. But your closest friend might just get a well-needed laugh out of the exact same parcel. There is a time, a place and a space for all of your care package themes, and the last thing you want is for your caring gesture to become a faux pas! So take the time to ponder before you post and have a good think about who is receiving the package, what they might need and how their package should look.

THIS WAY UP

I love you ♡

Is there a better reason to send a special parcel than love? Your nearest and dearest will be delighted to receive such a romantic gesture - and you're bound to have fun putting it together, too. Where other occasions might call for restraint, this is your chance to get super-creative and personal: the most romantic parcels contain surprises and memories, and can tell stories without words. Choose a theme and see where it takes you - anything goes, so long as you consider your love's favourite colours, scents, foods, hobbies and taste in music.

Instead of using a standard cardboard box to house your package, why not upcycle something that suits your loved one's personality, aesthetic or sense of humour? Milk crates, drawstring bags, wooden wine crates and biscuit tins all make great gift boxes. Perhaps he or she is not into material things? Bake some bread and wrap it up with homemade jam and freshly ground coffee or a favourite tea – a romantic breakfast for two!

If your object of affection is a little out of the box, get creative when it comes to presentation. You could turn your care package into a cryptic puzzle, with individually wrapped items. Tag one item with the number one and a clue to which parcel to open next. If your love adores mysteries, why not turn the whole thing into a treasure hunt for the location of the parcel? Each step of the journey could be rewarded with a small token or souvenir of your relationship (or chocolate!).

If it's a big statement you want to make, have the package delivered to their workplace or school for a seriously romantic public declaration (but make sure the recipient is not too shy and retiring to appreciate it).

Think of this as an opportunity to show just how much you know and care: whether the parcel is simple or elaborate, big or small, it should speak to who the recipient is, inside and out.

a handmade card
(see page 84)
or letter

a favourite
childhood toy or
book you've tracked
down online

a vintage copy of
their favourite
book with a
personalised cover

IDEAS FOR
INCLUSIONS

origami hearts
(see page 78)

a mix tape or USB
stick of memories
with personalised
artwork or tag

origami
photo book
(page 72)

an earth-shaped stress ball for relieving nerves

all these items are light and easy to post

Eggwhite Soap
Eiwit Zeep
with
Chamomile Flowers

Nordisk Vaseline
LIP BALM | ALOE VERA | MADE IN NORWAY

Away from home

I miss you

It's tough being away from friends and loved ones. Technology has made it a little easier, especially with FaceTime and Skype, but nothing makes up for time spent together.

If your loved one is far from home, a special delivery of their favourite things will go a long way to showing them how much they are missed. Go to town decorating the box on both the outside and inside! Get a group of your loved one's friends to compose a letter together. Write the lyrics of their favourite song in coloured pens on the inside of the box – and then fill it to the brim with all of the sights, sounds and tastes of home that they might be missing.

Never underestimate the power of cheesy address labels to bring a smile to a homesick person's face, either. Have fun addressing the parcel with over-the-top phrases like 'to the only person to make me laugh', 'to the super charming _____', 'to the unbelievably funny and clever _____', 'to the baby of the family' or 'to my super brainy brother/sister'.

Your parcel is guaranteed to put a smile on your loved one's face (and the postie's face, too) and make going to the mailbox a treat if it's seriously decorated and bursting with personality.

IDEAS FOR INCLUSIONS

anything local: newspaper clippings, magazines, or coasters from their favourite cafes or bars

handmade mini photo album (see pages 72–75) including photos of the people, pets and events they may be missing

a letter featuring paragraphs from their friends and family back home

favourite local snacks and treats

small items – a book, a trinket, a piece of jewellery or clothing – they may have left at home

I'm here for you

If something difficult is going on in your friend's life, a parcel is a great way to help them feel loved and get through tough times, especially if you can't be there in person to ease the disappointment, sorrow or heartache. You can choose to be practical or indulgent with this kind of care package but, as always, what you deliver will depend on your relationship with the recipient and his or her personality.

A complete parcel with everything needed to get through one meal of the day is a great practical idea. A breakfast parcel, for instance, could contain homemade muesli, fruit and yoghurt, freshly squeezed juice, ground coffee or loose-leaf tea. Lunch might include homemade soup, sandwiches with a variety of fillings, a healthy fruit loaf or some chocolate biscuits. Dinner options could be a hearty stew or risotto, pasta bake, homemade mini pies or a quiche. If you think your friend will be receiving lots of visitors at this time, an afternoon tea package may be the way to go. Try freshly baked scones, homemade jam and cream, a variety of baked biscuits or a lovely cake, and a selection of teas and some good-quality coffee.

If distance makes giving food unrealistic, or if you'd rather your care package be a little more indulgent, why not try a relaxation package including soothing music, bath salts and some cosy socks? Or give a DVD, popcorn and wine package and add yourself into the mix. Often, during hard times, people need company without the pressure of having to talk. You'll have to gauge how your friend is feeling here and art-direct a package just for them. Perhaps your package will include something from each of the ideas above!

IDEAS FOR INCLUSIONS

homemade meals

homemade treats (see pages 90–107)

something cosy, relaxing or soothing

movies that may put a smile on their face

art or colouring supplies for the creative recipient

a USB with music or podcasts with personalised artwork or tag (see pages 150–153)

magazines or a book of short stories

crossword and/or sudoku books

lavender oil and chamomile essential oils for relaxing baths and a good night's sleep

beautiful
handmade
crochet

home is
where the
heart is

handwritten
letter, drawings
and recipes from
every family
member

pretty
handmade
crochet wheel

THE ULMAN/EISNER FAMILY

Foxs Lane. Kate and Brendon, Vivienne, Indi, Jarrah and Pepper Daylesford, Australia

In our family, we have a tradition of giving and sending handmade gifts and packages. We believe that taking the time to truly think about the receiver – where they are, who they are, and what they might need and love – is as important a part of the process as putting together the package itself.

We send these parcels on all sorts of occasions, such as when someone important to us is far away, unwell or sad; or when they are celebrating, and we want to join in; or even when we just want to say, 'Hi, we're thinking of you.' It makes me happy to think that at these times we gather up the craft supplies rather than hitting the shops.

Some packages can be put together in an afternoon: a hand-drawn card, a batch of cookies, a carefully worded note and a sprinkling of confetti. Others can take weeks to come together: a pair of socks hand-knitted from the softest, squishiest wool in a colour the knitter enjoys knitting with and thinks the receiver will enjoy wearing, love and care knitted into each stitch.

And as we put it all together, we love to imagine the package arriving and being opened. The excitement upon receiving it at the post office; the wonder and guessing as its sender and shape and weight are considered; the excited ripping open of the outer layer to discover what's underneath; and the careful, quiet, slow lifting of each piece of tape or undoing of each knot.

Then, as they discover all that we have sent them, we hope that our giftee feels the love and care we have packaged up. That they understand what we intended. That they feel our wishes for them.

To receive a handmade gift in the mail is to receive a little bit of someone's heart.

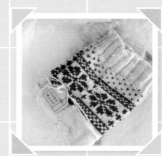

two bottles of
prosecco wrapped
in a furoshiki

see page 142 for
furoshiki wrapping
instructions

add a fabric
label made with
pinking shears

I want to spoil you

Has someone in your life been working hard, had a lot on his or her plate, or is a little snowed under for one reason or another? Help make the most of what little downtime your loved one has by putting together a pampering parcel - one of the loveliest surprise packages to receive.

While an air of luxury is what this package is all about, you certainly don't need to break the budget in order to infuse your gift with a certain *je ne sais quoi*. (In fact, the French know a thing or two about finding the luxury in the everyday! A chocolate croissant for breakfast, anyone? Lunch with a glass of wine?) Decorate your parcel in a limited colour palette so it looks simple and striking. Whether you opt for classic black and white or navy and cream, or a white box with an Yves Klein blue or shocking red ribbon, the aim is elegance. (Think French, of course!) For a deluxe personal touch, make custom labels featuring the recipient's name: _____'s foot scrub, _____'s chocolate biscuits, _____'s relaxing bath oils, _____'s woolly socks, _____'s cosy PJs.

Your care package could include a voucher for a massage or facial, a lunch voucher to a favourite cafe, or a babysitting voucher so the recipient can go out for a night on the town. Whatever you include, they should all be treats your loved one doesn't normally get. Indulgent doesn't have to mean expensive!

IDEAS FOR INCLUSIONS

for women: nail polish or lipstick in a new, modern colour

for men: a moisturiser or aftershave lotion especially for their skin type

homemade super-rich chocolate truffles (page 104)

a homemade pudding or dessert

a bottle of posh champagne

babysitting vouchers (see page 54)

a hamper with extravagant everyday items

cosy knitted socks

pyjamas or slippers

essential oils, bath bombs and body scrubs

homemade soap (page 76)

individual face masks

pop
typewritten
letters in
bags and wrap
around the
parcel

wrap
individual
items and roll
typewritten
letters in
scrolls

I want to thank you

I am a big believer in saying thank you. I don't think enough people say it, and I also think we are so unused to hearing it that it can come as a surprise to people when it's said to them. When someone is kind to you, or makes a difficult day nicer, saying thank you makes that person feel like the task was a pleasure, bringing the positive interaction full circle. So why not show people how much their kindness means to you?

You may want to thank hospital or medical staff, a boss, a family member or a friend. Or you may really want to say thank you for the unexpected kindness you received from a near stranger, a generous person you encounter every day, or a person that goes out of his or her way to do something lovely for you. Sometimes the person we want to thank may not have directly affected us but instead enriched our whole community, workplace or day-to-day life.

You might choose to put this package together with a group of friends, family or colleagues; if you are all crafty, handy or clever in the kitchen, you could each provide a homemade gift. Include a note describing what the recipient's kindness meant to you; if you're sending the package as a group, it gives you all the chance to articulate your message personally. You could attach helium balloons to the parcel and deliver it to the person's door or place of work, or decorate the wrapped package with fresh or dried flowers. Most importantly the package should look special, so however you choose to style it, be sure it makes an impact.

IDEAS FOR INCLUSIONS

a gigantic thank-you card to make the recipient feel super-spoilt

homemade chocolate truffles (page 104)

a bottle of wine or champagne

an Italian dinner package (page 197)

an afternoon tea package (page 207)

a mini terrarium

a cute pot-plant

a coffee- or tea-lover's package (pages 198 and 207)

I want to treat you

I feel lucky to have a few really close friends, an amazing husband and a lovely family. I don't ever take these people for granted; I think it's important to let people know how much you appreciate and care for them. There are lots of ways to do this, but a care package - just because - is a way to make the gift of friendship known.

Make and give this parcel to someone close to you just for being his or her wonderful self. It's an appreciation care package: you want to send a few small things that might brighten your loved one's day and hopefully return some of the happiness the recipient has brought to your life. Why not choose a date to spend the day together? When you agree on a time to meet up, send a package filled with small parcels, each containing a hint of one of your day's activities as a primer. Theme your day and give it a fun name: why not call it '_____ and _____'s excellent adventure' or '_____ and _____'s best day ever'? If you plan to do another one in the future, you could devise some movie or book series puns like The Girlfriends Strike Back (*Star Wars*) or The Pinot Noir of Azkaban (*Harry Potter*).

IDEAS FOR INCLUSIONS

fun and creative vouchers for a day out together (see page 54)

a breakfast, picnic, afternoon tea or Italian dinner care package (see pages 198, 196, 207 and 197)

a pampering package with bath salts, fluffy face flannel, face mask, moisturiser and hot water bottle

a cosy package (see page 194)

a coffee- or tea-lover's package (see pages 198 and 207)

homemade dinner delivery

small bags with
different treats
will delight

have fun
with your
presentation

As the saying goes, it's what's on the inside that counts. You don't need to spend a lot of money on lavish gifts to make somebody feel loved and cared for. An afternoon's worth of baking, a piece of paper ingeniously folded, music lovingly curated: all these won't break the bank, and yet they are some of the most wonderful inclusions to any care package. (Of course, sometimes, for the right person on the right occasion, you do just need to go all out!) In this chapter, you'll find some of my favourite items to gift to others. Pick and mix whatever takes your fancy, find inspiration and put your own personal spin on things for all of the people you love and cherish.

THIS WAY UP

Part and parcel

Materials

415

safety
pins

AVRIL

metal clips

plastic
buttons
and
stickers

confetti

wooden
buttons and
beads

pressed
flowers

coasters

peg
hooks

feathers and
pom poms

wooden
pegs

rosebud
tea and
dried
flora

craft shop
letters

beautifully
designed
stamps

muslin
bags

gold
and
silver
clips

fabric
buttons

paper
doilies

paper
clips

tags

linen
thread

daruma
thread

bright
photo
corners

ribbons

glassine
bags

wax paper
bags

paper
bags

plastic
twists

shredded paper
or eco bubble
wrap

coloured
cottons

paper
ephemera

calico

yarns and
twines

embroidery
threads

washi tapes

cellophane
bags

packing
tapes

Bound paper journals

once you get the hang of the technique, try making versions with more or fewer holes

I've used a Japanese twine that changes colour from teal to pink

flip a round tag or coaster and pencil in areas to pierce to make a threaded tag

if you want to use thicker twine, you'll need bigger holes in your paper

There are so many ways to make a personalised journal for your loved one. In high school, I used to spend days covering my writing books scrapbook-style with all my favourite band members and classic literature icons. A modern-day version of that old high-school tradition could work well, or try this beautifully simple hand-binding technique for a thoroughly elegant approach.

1 piece of thick A4 card for front and back of journal

scalpel, bone folder and cutting mat

15 pieces of A4 paper for internals, including optional recycled materials and/or letters and correspondence

bulldog clip, pencil and ruler

book binding awl (paper stabber)

needle and beautiful thread or fine twine of your choice

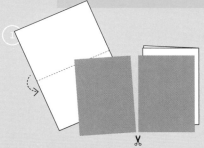

Take the piece of A4 card and cut it in half to make 2 × A5 pieces of card. Using a bone folder or the back of your scalpel to make sharp folds, fold the A4 paper pieces in half.

The holes are 2 cm (¾ in) apart and 1 cm (½ in) from the edge.

Sandwich the internal pages between the pieces of card, aligning the edges. Clamp together with a bulldog clip, placing it on the edge side of the journal, not the spine (fold) side. Mark in pencil the four places you will pierce holes.

Working on a cutting mat, use the book binding awl to pierce the four marked places all the way through the front cover, pages and back cover. Make sure the holes are big enough for your needle to go through.

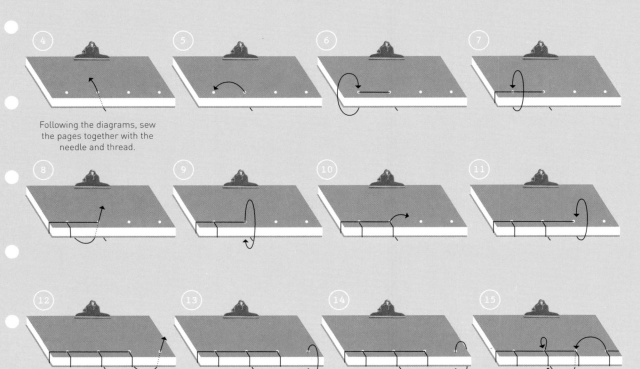

Following the diagrams, sew the pages together with the needle and thread.

Sew back into the last hole and tie a knot at the back to secure.

fold a pocket A6 journal cover

collage up pages of a store-bought journal for your loved one

Michelle Mackintosh

for a cute cover, paint dots onto watercolour paper

use office ring binders to hold your journal together

make it fun!

add envelopes and tabs

make a tag and hang it from your journal

stitch down the middle of your paper and cover

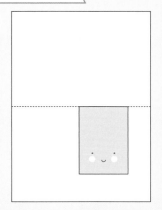

You'll need a piece of A3 paper and an A6 journal (or 10 × A5 pages stitched down the middle with a sewing machine). Fold the A3 sheet in half to make a rectangle the size of an A4 sheet of paper.

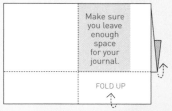

Make sure you leave enough space for your journal.

FOLD UP

Fold in half again to make a rectangle the size of an A5 sheet, then unfold. Align the journal as shown, then fold the excess paper at the bottom of the sheet up to make pockets.

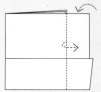

Fold the excess paper around the front and back of the journal to create flaps.

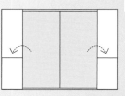

Tuck the front and back of the journal into the pocket flaps to secure the cover.

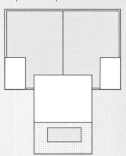

Decorate the pocket!

decorate journal pages as part of a travel pack (see page 177)

photobooks (see pages 72–75) and journals are best friends

CARE coupons

These cute vouchers are lovely to give on their own or as part of a larger care package. What you offer your friend or loved one is up to you - the one rule is that you must make good on what the coupon promises! Scan and print or photocopy the coupon of your choice onto nice thick card or, if you're feeling creative, use these vouchers as a starting point and invent your own. After all, you know your loved one best, and you'll have an idea of the very specific and personal things he or she will appreciate most.

This coupon entitles

_____ to...

☐ unlimited chat sessions over multiple cups of tea (or something stronger)

☐ a Netflix, chocolate and PJ disco house party

☐ one container of ice cream and a season of _____ to binge-watch together

☐ one bottle of wine, posh takeaway and someone to rant to

girlfriend
boyfriend
package

one foot massage, one bottle of champagne, one movie marathon, one homemade dinner and dessert – including dishes washed and house cleaned!

BFF
package

one BFF, one beautiful homemade dinner, more dessert than you can possibly eat

nature
package

one dose of nature, one picnic hamper, one frisbee, one disposable camera and one attentive listener

night
out
package

one group of best friends, one salon blow dry, one dinner at a favourite cafe, one night out on the town dancing and one cab ride home, with the optional extra of a midday breakfast with at least one Bloody Mary

road trip
package

one driver/singing partner/ excellent listener, an endless music selection, top-quality snacks, enthusiasm and lunch somewhere fun, kitsch or special

getaway
package

one weekend away at a mystery location, delicious food and favourite drinks, and possibly including campfires, walks on the beach, hikes in the mountains or dancing

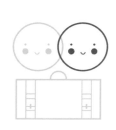

cheery
package

one pyjama party, endless snacks and one comedy marathon, and possibly including hugs, back rubs and hand holding

hospital package

call this number for an immediate visit:

_____

includes conversation, good company and the discretion to leave at a moment's notice, and possibly including magazines, books, one food parcel or one luxury hospital survival kit

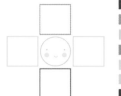

crafty package

all the supplies for an excellent crafternoon, including, of course, beautiful tea and homemade cake and a mix CD to set the mood

music package

a mix CD, USB full of music clips and documentaries, a karaoke partner, afternoon tea or dinner, and possibly including tickets to a show or bar/disco/club playing favourite songs

special
delivery

GUEST PACKAGE

sparkly USB

furoshiki
wrapping

hand
stitching

beautiful
handmade print

things to get
creative with

BECI ORPIN

Designer and author Melbourne, Australia

I made this care package for a girl called Chessie. Chessie is a sixteen-year-old blogger who has been following my work for a few years – I guess you could say she is a fan. She caught my attention a few years ago; she had to dress as a woman she admired for International Women's Day, and she chose to dress up as me! To say I was flattered is an understatement. After that, I started following her on Instagram. I admired her consistency and dedication to her blog – and her cute style, too.

It was also through Instagram that I discovered Chessie's mum tragically passed away from cancer. Chessie seemed to put on such a such a brave face, but I couldn't imagine what it would be like to lose a parent at any age, particularly at a time when you need your mum around the most. I had been thinking of sending Chessie something for quite some time, but these circumstances definitely got me cracking on the idea.

So I put together a package full of my favourite things that keep me happy and also creatively inspired. Chessie definitely has her own style and sensibilities, and a keen interest in design and fashion, so I guess I was hoping to help broaden her horizons a little in these fields, too.

I wrote a letter to explain the items in the package; each one relates either to one of her senses (for example, a USB stick containing my favourite music for her ears) or to something more abstract (like a magazine about up and coming creatives for her future).

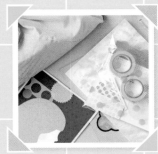

Fabric
journals

LEO

Fleischerei

enough pretty fabric and calico to wrap your journal with 3 cm (1¼ in) excess

enough iron-on adhesive to fuse your fabric pieces

an iron

needle and thread

buttons, ribbons or twine, to embellish

This is a really stylish way to pretty up a plain paper journal. I love to use linen or heavy cotton fabrics, stitch the edges and decorate with buttons, ribbon, twine or string. These journals don't need to be feminine: a strong, graphic print or a simple colour combination works really well for a unisex or more masculine design.

Open your journal up and place it on top of the pretty fabric and calico. Trace a shape roughly 1 cm (½ in) larger than the journal, with 3 cm (1¼ in) extra on the left and right sides to form flaps.

Sandwich the iron-on adhesive between the two fabrics, pin and trim to the same size. Follow the instructions of the iron-on adhesive to fuse the fabrics together.

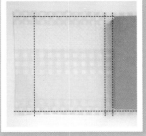

Measure and mark out the width and height of the spine, front and back of the journal, as well as the flaps. Align each part of the journal on the fabric to ensure it all fits. (This is crucial!)

Trim to size, making sure you leave 1 cm (½ in) at the top and bottom of the journal cover to prevent frayed edges. Iron down the flaps and the excess at the top and bottom.

Wrap around the journal, making sure everything fits snugly.

Hem the top and bottom edges of the journal cover with a needle and thread. Stitch a button to the front of the journal and wrap twine or ribbon around it to secure and finish.

Origami CD cover

A4 black and white design template page 232

this CD cover looks a little like a kimono

use the same paper design for other elements in your care package, like chocolate!

using permanent markers, draw your chosen design onto a blank CD

HOME MADE

template (page 232) design printed onto A4 paper (or your own design)

blank CDs
your music collection

permanent markers
tags to decorate (optional)

A thoughtfully curated CD, USB stick or analogue mix tape is one of my favourite care package inclusions. You simply can't buy this in stores! Mix tapes require a lot of thought about the recipient's taste in pop-culture, art and politics. If you already know some of the recipient's favourite songs, why not throw in a few left-of-centre selections, theme it to their interests, or include a secret track or voice recording? Research something from another era that has the same feel as one of their current favourites or include a musician who has influenced their favourite band. Mix-tape artwork, like this fun origami CD cover, will swiftly take cues from your mix and fall into place.

Align the top margin of the A4 paper with the centre of the CD.

Fold the left and right sides of the paper to enclose the CD.

Fold the bottom of the paper where the white design starts.

Open back up and make a diagonal fold as shown.

Pinch to form a second fold and flatten as shown.

Repeat on the opposite side.

Place the CD into the upper folds to secure.

Fold over the flap and mark where the cover and base join.

Fold the top corners down and tuck into the bottom of the cover.

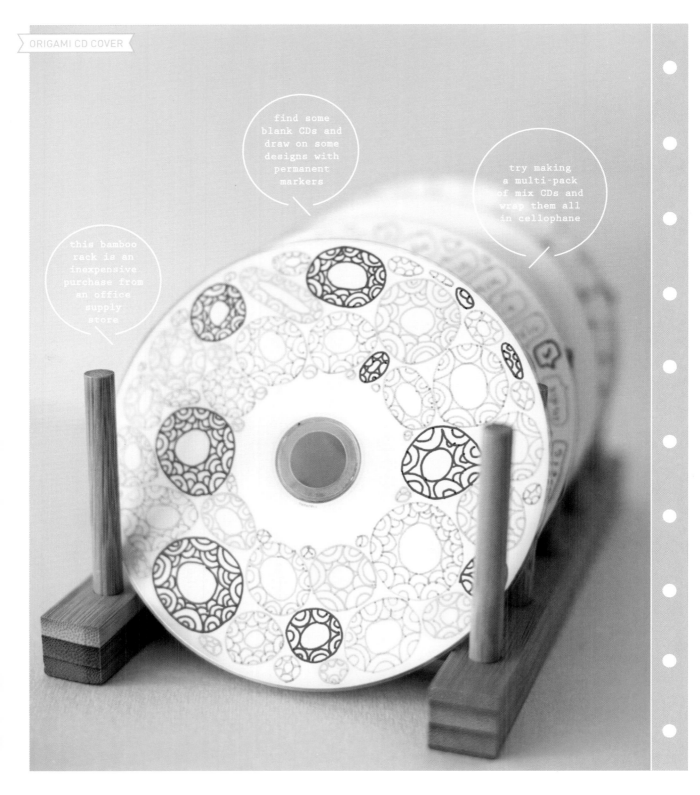

> "Charity begins at home, and justice begins next door."
>
> Charles Dickens

use a stamp in the middle of a rosette

stamp onto calico

experiment with new colour palettes

try designing your own stamp and taking it to a maker

make a card out of a rubber stamp design

Rubber stamps

I'm a huge fan of rubber stamps. You can use them over and over again and experiment by stamping onto different sorts of fabrics, papers and recycled materials. I love making labels and tags by stamping onto calico and hand-stitching edges.

On page 69, you can find some stamps I've designed for you to take to a professional stamp-maker (it's a relatively inexpensive exercise), as well as some designs that you can carve yourself, using an eraser or a rubber sheet from your local art supply. It takes a little bit of confidence and practice, but once you get going, it's highly addictive and oh-so-therapeutic. My stamp-maker, Paper Pastries in California, makes the most beautiful-quality wooden stamps out of my designs. I must confess to dreaming up new designs all the time and then somehow justifying having them made.

Rubber stamps are also a great way to link all the items in your care package with your personal wrapping style. You can change string, ribbon, box, ink and paper colours for different people in your life, so no two packages will ever look the same. Visit your local art or craft shop for some interesting ink colours and investigate buying fabric inks if you are thinking of stamping onto fabric.

stamp onto pages from old books, cut out shapes and layer up with coloured papers

make some letter art to include in your package, along with a variety of rubber stamp designs

Decorating calico bags

make a woodland design on your bag using different coloured inks

why not stitch a simple fabric design onto calico?

To carve your own stamps, you'll need to visit your art supply store to buy a carving or linocut tool set suitable for rubber, as well as some rubber blocks (or else you can carve your design into erasers). Trace or draw your design onto the rubber and, with your tool nearly parallel to the surface, start carving. Use a larger tool to carve away the edges. Be careful as carving tools are very sharp!

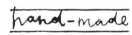

special delivery

GUEST PACKAGE

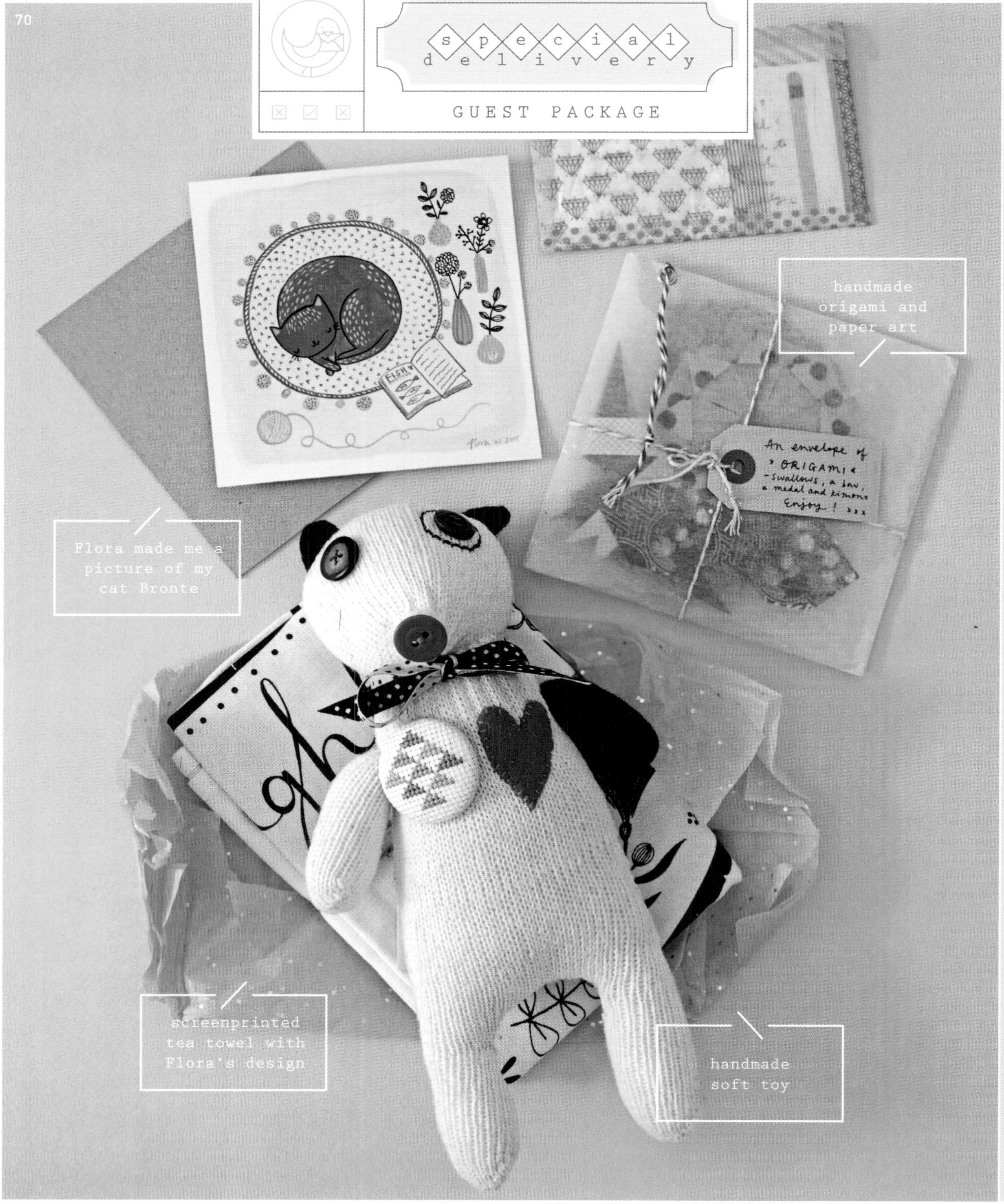
handmade origami and paper art
Flora made me a picture of my cat Bronte
An envelope of ORIGAMI - swallows, a bow, a medal and kimono Enjoy! xxx
screenprinted tea towel with Flora's design
handmade soft toy

FLORA WAYCOTT

Illustrator and designer Wellington, New Zealand (by way of the UK and Japan)

The first time I moved countries was in 1988, when I was six years old. I was born in the UK to an English father and a Japanese mother, and they had decided to move us to Japan in order for my sister and I to learn the language and culture while we were still very young.

After five wonderful years, we moved back to England, leaving our life in Japan behind. It was during my time at school in Japan that I developed a love of stationery and gift-giving, and vowed to my friends that we would all stay in touch via frequent letters and packages. This carried on for many years, in particular with my best friend Kunie, who would send me packages containing the latest fads in Japan: stationery with the latest cute characters, purikura (little photobooth photos), hair bands and mix tapes of her favourite Japanese bands. In our teens we would send each other more grown-up presents, like make-up and jewellery. We would correspond in Japanese, later on switching to English as she practised for her high school English exams. She came to visit me in England when we were sixteen, her first overseas trip, and would frequently write to me about how much she enjoyed the trip for some time after she left. Sadly, she passed away when we were eighteen, but I hope that we would have still been sending each other packages today.

I went to live in Japan again when I was 21 to study at a textile school in Kyoto and in 2008 I moved again, this time to live in New Zealand. My family are spread apart (my parents in England and my sister in Tokyo) and my friends are now scattered around the world, so staying in touch with loved ones through written correspondence and sending care packages feels very personal and precious to me. I love opening my letter box to find a package that someone has put together just for me. That they have taken the time to select something nice, sit down and write a letter, and go to the post office to post it always makes me feel as though I am not so far away.

Origami
photo
book

Photo books are one of the most personal items to include in a care package. They come in many forms, as you will see over the next few pages, but I am quite partial to the simple charm of this origami version. So gather up all of the best memories you can find and sort into a lovely package to remind your loved one of unforgettable moments. Collaging up a shared memory bank is a wonderful way to connect you with others and will be a treasured personal item for years to come.

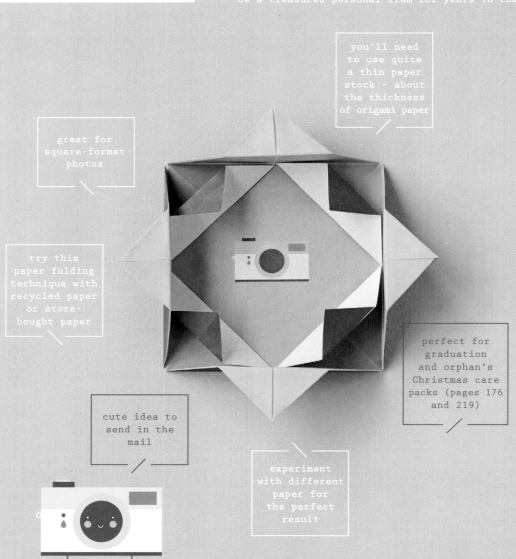

you'll need to use quite a thin paper stock - about the thickness of origami paper

great for square-format photos

try this paper folding technique with recycled paper or store-bought paper

perfect for graduation and orphan's Christmas care packs (pages 176 and 219)

cute idea to send in the mail

experiment with different paper for the perfect result

Outside of origami photo book (see template, page 228)

Insert for inside of origami photo book (see template, page 229)

(1)

With the wrong (white) side of the paper facing up, fold the four corners of the paper so that they meet in the middle.

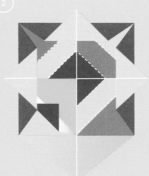

(2)

Fold along the dotted white lines shown in the diagram on the far left, following the fold directions indicated in the diagram on the near left.

(3)

Slip the insert into the centre of the origami photo book.

(4)

FRONT

Fill the photo book with photos, then seal the back with a sticker or wrap with twine.

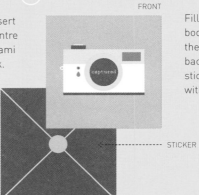

STICKER

Photo book ideas

use vintage
paper corners
to fix photos
to thick
cotton paper

Tokyo 2015

personalise with
a rubber stamp
letter set

try using an
analogue camera
and processing

perfect
for away-from-home
packages
(pages 156-165)

wrap photos
in patterned
greaseproof
paper and bind
with twine,
beads and
washi tape

cut
natural board into
old-fashioned tag
shapes and ring-bind

use a
permanent
marker to
draw a
vintage
camera
onto your
muslin bag

buy some
bright and fun
photo corners
online

Melt-and-pour soap

package finished soap in wax paper and string, rubber-stamped brown paper bags, muslin bags, baking paper and ribbon, or tiny boxes

make labels listing the scent, texture and therapeutic benefits

I've used vintage sewing patterns to pad out the box

try setting your soap in different shapes

buy some special moulds online, or use anything from a cut-down milk carton to an ice-cream container

cut the soaps with rough edges for a super-handmade feel

450 g (1 lb) melt-and-pour soap base (available online or at health food stores)

soap moulds or a cake tin lined with baking paper

½ tablespoon of neutral or essential oil of your choice, plus any extra additions as desired

Making soap the traditional way is a bit of a tricky business, and not a suitable activity for children due to the use of caustic soda. However, making soap from a melt-and-pour base, soap flakes or small pieces of leftover soap can be a wonderful afternoon project for all ages – and, when finished, will still look incredibly impressive. There are many fantastic online stores that specialise in base products and all of the additives you will need; however, if you have a lovely garden or a cupboard full of oils, salts, seeds and spices, you may already have half the ingredients you need. This is a great project that allows you to get creative with colour, texture and scent. And, once you've finished, packaging the soaps adds another dimension full of creative possibilities.

Cut your soap base into 1.5 cm (½ in) cubes and place in a large, oven-safe glass bowl. Microwave the soap base for 30 seconds, then for intervals of 15 seconds, stirring between bursts and checking to see when it is melted. Soap can burn, so keep an eye on it.

I like to make each soap a little different, so when the soap base is melted, I stir through the essential oil and divide it between several smaller bowls, then add any extra additions (for instance, coffee or poppy seeds). Pour the soap into the mould and decorate the tops if desired (I pop a whole coffee bean on my coffee-scented soap). If making several varieties of soap, try layering one on top of another for a lovely layered effect. Use a rounded knife or spatula to get rid of any small bubbles on top before the soap starts to set.

Remove the soap from the moulds after a couple of hours. Place onto a cake rack and leave overnight. Wrap beautifully and add to your care package or store in an airtight container until you assemble your package.

TIP You can try this with soap flakes or grated leftover soap, but you may need to add a little cow, almond or soy milk to soften and help the flakes combine. Add 185 ml (6 fl oz/ ¾ cup) of milk to 450 g (1 lb) of soap and leave overnight before melting.

TIP When storing soaps in an airtight container, use a layer of baking paper to separate them.

TIP A variety of soap bases is available. I like to use ones made from glycerine, shea butter and olive oil.

Optional extras

for exfoliation: salt, coffee, sugar, poppy seeds, almond meal

for deodorisation: coffee

for visual effect: dried lavender, mint, rosemary or thyme, poppy seeds

for moisturisation (start with a tablespoon; too much will prevent your soap from setting): aloe vera, shea butter, coconut oil, beeswax

storage: boxes and all forms of wrapping

delivery: all forms, including mail

use by: 6 months

Origami mobiles

type up a letter
and fold into an
origami heart

cut
washi tape
into flags

perfect
for a mother and
baby pack (page 170)

mix
vintage papers
with brights

pop
secret notes
under each flap in
the back of your hearts

origami paper and squares of recycled or vintage paper | washi tape, natural twine | a cute clothes hanger (wooden, vintage or a cute shape like this cloud)

Origami mobiles are a wonderful way to brighten up a room and bring a little colour into someone's life. While these would be perfect for a mother and baby pack (page 170), I do think they are a lovely gift for all ages. You can also fold individual hearts and stars and use them as accents in your packages.

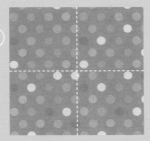

(1) Fold the square into quarters and unfold.

(2) Turn over. Fold the bottom edge up to the middle fold, then turn over again.

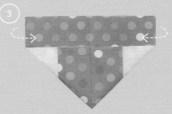

(3) Fold the bottom corners so they meet in the centre. Turn over again.

(4) Fold the sides so they meet in the centre.

(5) Fold in the top left and right corners to form a peak. Without folding, carefully bring the top point down to meet the bottom point.

(6) Carefully flatten to create two inward-pointing triangles at the top of the shape. Fold down the top right and top left corners.

(7) Tuck the front point of the heart into the pocket behind it.

(8) Fold down the top points and flip over to complete the heart shape!

Tape twine to the back of the hearts and affix to the hanger with washi tape.

With the wrong side facing up, fold each piece of paper diagonally and open back up.

Fold in half as shown, so the right side of the paper is now facing up. Open the paper back up.

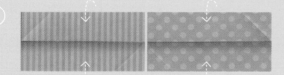

Fold the top and bottom edges in to meet the centre crease.

Turn the paper 180° and fold in half as shown.

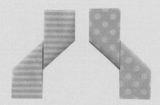

Following the existing diagonal crease in the paper, fold the bottom edge up so it meets the centre crease. Fold the top edge down to meet the centre crease.

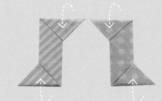

Flip the pieces over. Fold the top and bottom peaks as shown.

Fold down the bottoms and tops to make the shapes shown. Allow the bottoms and tops to unfold.

Flip the right shape over and position the two pieces as shown. Lay the left piece on top of the right piece so the vertical edges run parallel to the right shape's folds.

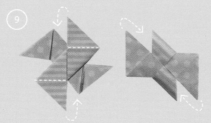

Fold the top shape at the dotted lines and tuck the points into the pockets at the back of the bottom shape.

Fold and tuck the points of the bottom shape into the pockets of the top shape. Voilà!

Postal tea bags

I love rose tea and Turkish delight together

try using vintage stamps with a design or subject your friend will love

a pencil and pinking shears
loose-weave muslin
(cheesecloth)

good-quality loose leaf tea
(I've used rose tea)

uncoloured natural twine
vintage postal stamps

A cup of hot tea in a favourite chair is one of the simplest stress-relievers one could possibly ask for. These homemade tea bags can be customised to suit anyone's taste in tea, and a parcel containing these personalised infusions is like a delivery of peace and tranquility.

Using a pencil, draw circles approximately 16 cm (6¼ in) in diameter onto the muslin (I used an overturned breakfast bowl as a template). Using pinking shears, cut out the circles. Place a small amount of tea (about 1 teaspoon, see example opposite, or use the recommended amount for one cup according to the packet) into the centre of each muslin circle.

For each circle, gather up the edges into the centre and bunch into a neat shape. Tie with twine to secure the tea, leaving enough twine to drape over the edge of a cup and for you to attach the postage stamp labels. Choose two matching stamps and sandwich the twine between them. And there you have it! Perfectly pretty handmade tea bags, just right for any tea-loving friend's care package.

because they are so pretty, I like to package my tea bags in something translucent or transparent

storage: tins, jars, bags, cellophane

delivery: bicycle, walking or car

use by: 6 months

Cards
and paper
additions

a great care
package for a
friend who is
writing a book
or studying

collage up
a paper-cut
design onto
the front of a
store-bought
journal

pop the
journal into
a muslin bag
with decorated
tags

buy a ruler
and pen in your
colour palette
to add to the
package

15 FEBRUARY

C.E. WHITT

DELFONICS

collage up some brown recycled paper for a quick and effective card design

fold your hearts in half and glue half onto the card

try a simple watercolour design on cotton or handmade paper

try a repeat pattern and change up the faces

CONGRATS

mini congratulations flag template page 229

cat designs are always appropriate!

Beci made a BS collage

Beci and Alice made an Otto cushion for Arro Homewares

Miso is our BS senior

Michelle printed Bronte onto canvas

Alice decorated cat food

Ari made a green BS

Alice art directed cat nip

Bronte's Cat Nip ~100% NATURAL~

Adeline made pom pom BSC members

Alice made a laser-cut Bronte and Beci made a pom pom toy

水曜日 SUIYOUBI

TOP CAT

Michelle art directed biscuits

Steve and Michelle made a BSC mix tape

Chester is the baby of the BSC

THE BRITISH SHORTHAIR CLUB

*British shorthair fanciers Michelle Mackintosh, Steve Wide, Beci Orpin, Alice Oehr and Adeline Kurniadjaja,
owners of Bronte, Tio and Miso, Otto, Humphrey (RIP), and Chester* Melbourne, Australia

Steve, Beci, Alice, Adeline and I all own British shorthair cats. To say we are obsessed with this breed would be a bit of an understatement. We are classic cat fanciers: we know the history of the breed and what to look out for when spotting a great specimen. We all have Instagram accounts that feature our shorthairs heavily (Steve and Adeline are the worst offenders here). Our little beasts are admired by people on all continents and we regularly spot and @ each other when we come across a beautiful BS with classic features or unusual colours.

We are always looking out for new and interesting craft projects to make at our BS Club meetings. There is always a lot of inspiration on both Pinterest and Instagram for small knitted jumpers, handmade toys, cute cat bowls and the like.

We thought it would be lovely to get together and make a care package for a cat or kitten arrival. We each chose an activity and a project to add to the package.

Our animals are as important as any human friend or family member. We hope these pictures provide inspiration next time you have a friend who is expecting a new furry addition.

Michelle Mackintosh

Homemade bath salts

experiment with beautiful colours and textures

130 g (4½ oz/1 cup)
Epsom salts

40 g (1½ oz/⅓ cup) pink sea salt

10 g (⅓ oz/½ cup) food-safe
dried rosebuds or rose petals
(available at specialty tea shops)

16 g (½ oz/½ cup) green loose-
leaf tea (I've used genmaicha)

A hot bath is a wonderful escape from the stresses of daily life. Magnesium sulfate, more commonly known as Epsom salts, can help soothe sore muscles and ease the tension of the day away - perfect for anyone you think could use a break!

In a bowl, combine the Epsom salts and pink sea salt. Divide the mixture into two, and add the rosebuds or petals to one half and the green loose-leaf tea to the other. Package to your liking; stamped calico drawstring bags are one of my favourite ways to gift bath salts.

You might like to replace the rosebuds or green tea with other additions, such as a couple of drops of lavender (for relaxation) or peppermint (for reinvigoration) essential oil, or skin-beautifying ingredients like powdered milk, honey or almond oil.

dried lavender
is also a
wonderful bath
salt additive

storage: box, muslin or
paper bag or cellophane

delivery: bicycle,
walking or car

use by: 6 months

450 g (1 lb) mashed banana

1 apple, finely sliced (skin on or off according to your preference)

100 g (3½ oz) sultanas (golden raisins)

zest of 1 lemon

50 g (1¾ oz/½ cup) walnuts (or your favourite nut), roughly chopped

100 ml (3½ fl oz) vegetable oil

4–6 tablespoons almond or soy milk

75 g (2½ oz/¾ cup) rolled oats

75 g (2½ oz/½ cup) plain (all-purpose) flour, plus extra for dusting

75 g (2½ oz/½ cup) self-raising flour

I love this loaf, which just so happens to be vegan and free of refined sugar. It's easy to make and is delicious for breakfast or with a cup of tea in the afternoon. When I serve this to friends, they are always astounded when I say it contains no added sugar: the fruit gives the loaf the perfect amount of sweetness. This is ideal for a friend recovering from illness, for it tastes wonderful while being healthier than the average cake, and is brilliant if you're thinking of making a loved one an afternoon tea package. If you're putting something together for a friend who is swamped with work and has children, it will be appreciated as a delicious addition to lunch boxes. If you substitute the flour with gluten-free flour, you'll have a refined sugar-free, gluten-free, vegan treat that's difficult to beat!

Preheat your oven to 190°C (370°F).

In a large bowl, mix all of the ingredients except the flours together, until well combined. I usually do this with my hands, as I find it's quicker and more effective, though mixing with a spoon is perfectly acceptable.

Sift the flours into the bowl and carefully fold into the wet mixture with a rubber spatula or large spoon, until just combined. Take care here, as the density and texture of your cake depends on how gentle you are with your mixture: the lighter your hand when you mix, the lighter your cake

Grease the inside of a 25 cm × 11 cm (10 in × 4¼ in) loaf (bar) tin with a little vegetable oil, then dust with plain flour until the bottom and sides of the tin are coated. Tip the excess flour out. Line the bottom of the tin with baking paper and spoon in the mixture. Bake for 40 minutes, or until a skewer inserted into the centre of the cake comes out clean. Transfer to a baking rack to cool for 10 minutes. Remove the cake from the tin and allow to cool completely on the rack. Wrap in baking paper, tie with twine and add to your care package.

storage: airtight tin or Tupperware

delivery: bicycle, walking or car

use by: 1 week

Sugar cookies

HOME MADE

rolled-out dough can be layered between sheets of baking paper, double-wrapped in cling film and frozen for 4-6 weeks before thawing and baking

these biscuits are perfect sandwiched together with Nutella, lemon curd (page 100) or icing and jam

| 1 egg, lightly beaten | 1 teaspoon vanilla essence | 2 teaspoons baking powder |
| 225 g (8 oz) softened butter, cubed | 200 g (7 oz) caster (superfine) sugar | 415 g (14½ oz/2¾ cups) plain (all-purpose) flour |

I am completely addicted to making cut-out biscuits (or cut-out cookies, as my American friends know them). I travel to Japan regularly and never come home without a new cookie cutter. Kappabashi-dori (also known as Kitchen Town) in Tokyo is a long street in Asakusa devoted to kitchenware. It's a dream destination for the home cook or baker, where you'll find cookie cutters in hundreds of different shapes and sizes. I often spend a day making a double batch of this recipe for Christmas presents, parties or multiple care packages. Once these biscuits have been integrated into your baking regime, you'll find so many new and interesting ways to cut and decorate them. My favourite cookie cutter shape at the moment is my fat British Shorthair cat one (see page 95): I can make my own Bronte-shaped biscuits, which is just about my favourite thing to do.

Preheat your oven to 200°C (390°F). Line a baking tray with baking paper and set aside.

In a large bowl, rub the softened butter into the sugar with your fingertips until combined, then beat with an electric mixer on medium speed until the mixture turns pale.

Add the vanilla essence to the egg and stir to combine. Beat the egg mixture into the butter mixture a little at a time; it's important to do this bit by bit so the batter doesn't curdle.

Sift the flour and baking powder into the bowl and, using a rubber spatula, fold into the wet mixture until combined. Once the dough has come together, transfer it to a lightly floured work surface and divide into two balls. Set one ball aside and flatten the other with the palm of your hand. Lightly dust your rolling pin with flour and roll out the dough until it is 5 mm (¼ in) thick. Cut the dough into shapes with your cookie cutters. Transfer the biscuits to the lined baking tray and set aside the dough scraps. Repeat with the second dough ball.

Gather up all of the dough scraps and form into a ball. Flatten with the palm of your hand, roll out with your rolling pin and cut into squares. Transfer to the baking tray – these biscuits are perfect for keeping hungry mouths and biscuit thieves at bay if you are baking for a specific occasion.

Bake the biscuits for 6–8 minutes, until the palest shade of gold. You do not want your biscuits to brown; for best results, stay close to the oven and check the biscuits' progress after 5 minutes. Transfer to a wire rack to cool completely before decorating.

The icing (frosting) and decorating stage is where you can be most creative! I often use a pre-made 'paint-style' icing product to pipe my decoration onto the biscuits – this saves on time and cleanup. You can of course whip up your own icing and pipe it with a traditional bag and a nozzle size that is right for your design.

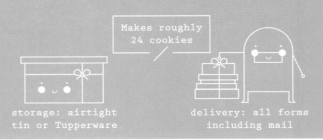

Makes roughly 24 cookies

storage: airtight tin or Tupperware

delivery: all forms including mail

use by: 1 week

pack together or as separates

I've drawn on biscuits with an icing pen

try animal shapes

purrrfect for a feline loving friend!

use a cookie letter set to personalise

package with buttons and paper clips

CARE PACKAGE

add cute labels

HOME MADE

great for sick kids or children's charities

package in cellophane bags

make washi tape flags with toothpicks

special delivery

GUEST PACKAGE

handmade
colouring book

handmade
paper flowers

hand-painted
wrapping paper

MAGDALENA FRANCO

Crafter, maker, mama and Head Honcho at Unleash Creative Brisbane, Australia

I have cracked a wicked grin many times when I've received a parcel in my letterbox, or better yet, when it has required the importance of the postman (or woman) hand-delivering it to me personally. Knowing that someone has taken time out of their day to think about me, shop or make something especially for me and then the added effort of going to the post office sure makes me feel special – even more so when it's an unexpected 'just because' parcel.

My dear friend Donna moved to Nashville, Tennessee over a decade ago. We were both single when we became friends. We have since found and married a couple of good guys, had two small humans each and led very separate lives. But despite the length of time that has passed since we last saw each other (when Donna married her guy six years ago), we have continued to stay in touch via phone calls, Skype catch-ups and care packages.

These care packages are something we both look forward to immensely. Neither of us ever knows when to expect the next parcel, which makes it all the more exciting and spontaneous. We take turns sending each other a box containing things such as favourite foods (she misses Vegemite and Cadbury Crunchies, so they are a must in almost every parcel I send to her), delicious teas, soaps, accessories, cute stationery, handmade items, and clothing and toys for each other's small people.

I adore receiving objects from other countries, especially when those items are synonymous with their country of origin. An example is America's famous range of chocolates and candy, particularly the ones that you can't readily find in Australia. Receiving them reminds me of so many great holidays to the US.

Homemade muesli

100 g (3½ oz/1 cup) rolled oats
40 g (1½ oz/⅓ cup) slivered almonds

40 g (1½ oz/⅓ cup) sultanas or dried cranberries, or a mix of both

30 g (1 oz/¼ cup) goji berries
4 dried pear halves, diced

A good breakfast is a great start to the day, especially if it has been made and delivered with love. You can play around with the dried fruits and nuts in this recipe - toasted hazelnuts, sunflower seeds and sesame seeds are all delicious, or omit nuts completely if your recipient is allergic - and a teeny amount of cinnamon, if desired, is a surefire way to spice things up!

Combine all ingredients in a bowl and package to your liking.

For a decadent toasted variation, heat 1 tablespoon each of honey, brown sugar and rice bran oil in a small saucepan. Stir until the sugar has dissolved, then pour over the combined ingredients. Mix well, spread on a lined baking tray and bake in a preheated 150°C (300°F) oven, stirring every 10 minutes, until golden brown. Allow to cool completely before packaging.

this delicious muesli is gluten-free!

storage: glass jars

delivery: bicycle, walking or car

use by: 1 week

Lemon curd

include some lemons (even better if they are from your garden) in your care package

sandwich sugar cookies (page 92) with lemon curd

dip sponge fingers (savoiardi) biscuits in lemon curd (see Italian pack page 197)

3 eggs
100 g (3½ oz) unsalted butter

juice and zest of 2½ lemons
150 g (5½ oz) sugar

My husband Steve and I planted lemon trees in our tiny courtyard. Every year there is an abundance of lemons that we love to give to friends and family to use. Steve is a pretty impressive pastry cook and loves to make jars of curd from the lemons in our garden. In fact, this is our most favourite dessert! When we got married, we chose the venue for a small party based on the chef's lemon tart (which we had in lieu of a wedding cake). I always think that when something is made especially for you, it tastes ten times better than when you make it yourself. When it's not dolloped into mini pastries, we like to dunk Italian savoiardi into it. A jar of curd and some neatly packaged cookies (with or without a mini bottle of prosecco) is a lovely care package on its own - or include it as part of the Italian pack (see page 197).

In a bowl, lightly whisk the eggs and pass through a fine mesh strainer to remove any lumps.

Combine the butter, lemon juice, zest and sugar in a saucepan over low heat. Stir until all of the butter has melted and the sugar has dissolved, then remove from the heat.

Reduce the heat to very low. Whisk the eggs into the butter mixture and return the saucepan to the heat, whisking constantly until the curd thickens. Do not allow it to come to a boil; this will curdle the mixture. Remove the saucepan from the heat once

more and pour the curd into sterilised jars.

For a variation on this simple recipe, simply substitute any other citrus fruit for the lemons (taking size into account, of course). Blood orange curd and ruby red grapefruit curd are two of my favourites.

If you have a lemon tree, press some lemon flowers to go with your care package

storage: glass jars

delivery: bicycle, walking or car

use by: 2 weeks

Roasted tomato sauce

mix with a tin of cannellini, lima or haricot (navy) beans for homemade fancy baked beans

stuff in a baguette with fior di latte cheese and fresh basil leaves

on the label or tag, give your friend some serving suggestions for the roasted tomatoes

spoon through your favourite cooked pasta and top with parmesan

10 roma (plum) tomatoes, halved lengthways

olive oil, for drizzling

balsamic vinegar, for drizzling

3 garlic cloves, unpeeled

5 basil leaves, torn in two, plus extra whole leaves for bottling

When my friend May was pregnant, I would sometimes leave a fresh jar of this delicious sauce on her doorstep as a quick dinner solution. It's technically a pasta sauce, but half an hour after I had dropped it off at May's, she would message me to say she had eaten it warm, straight out of the jar! So, while this tomato sauce is perfect for pasta, or for adding to a tin of beans to make fancy baked beans (which I love dolloped on toast with a little parmesan), don't let that limit your kitchen creativity. Did I mention it's vegan, too?

Preheat your oven to 160°C (320°F). Pop your tomato halves into a lined baking dish and season well with salt and pepper. Pour a generous glug of olive oil over each tomato, then follow suit with about one-third of the amount of balsamic. Mix the tomatoes, oil and vinegar together with your hands, then add the garlic cloves and top each tomato half with a basil leaf half. Roast for an hour, checking every 20 minutes and rotating the dish to ensure even cooking, if necessary. Remove from the oven and allow to cool.

When the tomatoes have cooled, spoon into a clean glass jar (or jars), adding a few extra basil leaves to the sauce, preferably where they can be seen. Fasten the lid and have fun decorating the jar, or make it a label or tag to match your care package. This will last up to a week in your refrigerator – if you don't eat it before then!

Serves 2 as a pasta sauce for dinner

use as a condiment to go with your favourite meat or vegetable dish

storage: glass jars

delivery: bicycle, walking or car

use by: 1 week

250 g (9 oz) high-quality dark chocolate, chopped

170 ml (5½ fl oz/⅔ cup) cream (35% fat content or greater)

1 tablespoon glucose syrup, light corn syrup or mild honey

20 g (¾ oz) unsalted butter, at room temperature

good-quality unsweetened cocoa, for rolling

Homemade chocolate truffles are such an impressive addition to a care package, even if they are super-simple to make! While this recipe uses dark chocolate for the base and cocoa for rolling, you can also substitute milk or white chocolate and decorate however you please - crushed toasted hazelnuts for milk chocolate or chopped pistachios for white are some of my favourites. These truffles do melt easily, so they are best hand-delivered or couriered - unless you are posting them in a very cold climate!

Place the chopped chocolate in a large, heatproof bowl.

In a small saucepan over low heat, bring the cream and glucose syrup to a simmer. Remove from the heat and pour over the chopped chocolate. Allow to stand for 15 seconds, then, with a rubber spatula or wooden spoon, carefully incorporate the hot cream and chocolate to make a ganache. Add the butter and stir through the ganache until it is completely dissolved and the ganache is smooth and glossy.

Cover the bowl with cling film and place in the refrigerator for 10–20 minutes, or until the ganache is partly set and able to be rolled into balls. Remove from the refrigerator and, using a teaspoon, scoop out balls of ganache and place on a tray covered with baking paper. Alternatively, you can transfer the ganache to a piping bag and pipe balls directly onto the tray. Place the tray in the refrigerator to allow the ganache balls to harden up.

To decorate, sift the cocoa onto a plate and, working quickly so the chocolate doesn't melt and stick to your hands, roll the ganache balls in the cocoa to make rustic truffles. Store in the refrigerator until you are ready to package them up.

make sure you buy good-quality ingredients for this recipe

storage: cellophane bags or a tin

delivery: bicycle, walking or car

use by: 1 month

Chocolate truffles

add the seeds scraped from a vanilla bean to the cream for vanilla-scented truffles

add a dash of liqueur to the cream for grown-up truffles

roll white-chocolate truffles in crumbled freeze-dried raspberries

HOME MADE

this chocolatey treat is rich so you only need to package them in small amounts

add grated orange zest to the ganache for a wonderful choc-orange flavour

Cold pressed juice

I have a cold-press juicer at home and love to make fresh juices for friends who are unwell. My husband Steve and I always research their conditions, make up special concoctions, bottle them up in recycled or new containers, prettify and deliver. Here are a few of our favourites. Have fun experimenting with your own colour and flavour combinations. There are so many wonderful vegetables packed full of vitamins and nutrients to experiment with.

Relaxation juice	Antioxidant juice	Breathe-easy juice	Anti-inflammatory juice
½ small cucumber	150 g (5½ oz)	5 carrots	5 carrots
½ pineapple	raspberries	2 oranges	4 celery sticks
1 green apple	(frozen or fresh)	1 apple	2 green apples
1 small piece ginger	1 handful blueberries	1 cucumber	1 small piece ginger
5 kale leaves	2 carrots	1 celery stick	1 small piece turmeric
1 celery stick	1 green apple		
squeeze of lemon juice	1 pear		

storage: glass jars

delivery: bicycle, walking or car

use by: 1 week

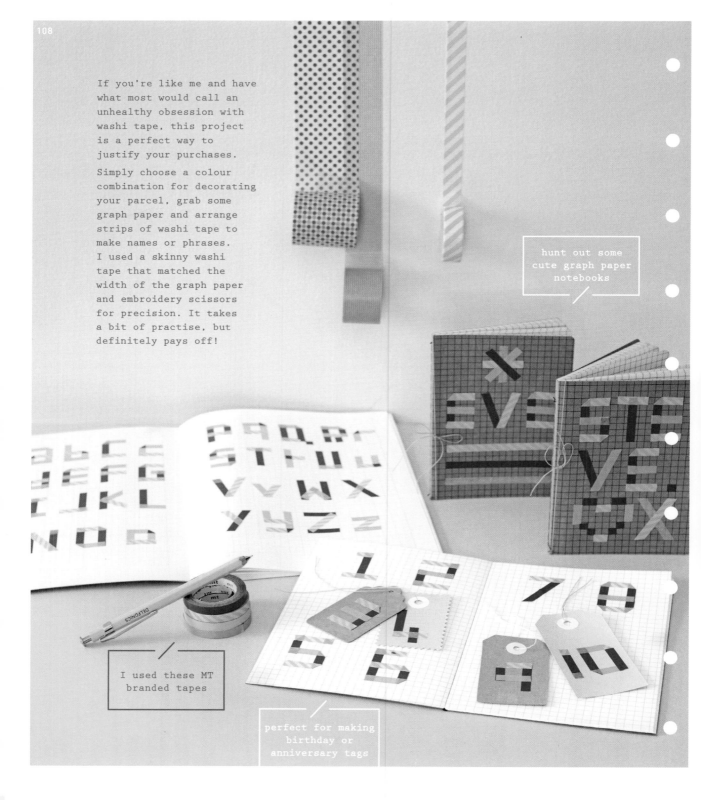

If you're like me and have what most would call an unhealthy obsession with washi tape, this project is a perfect way to justify your purchases.

Simply choose a colour combination for decorating your parcel, grab some graph paper and arrange strips of washi tape to make names or phrases. I used a skinny washi tape that matched the width of the graph paper and embroidery scissors for precision. It takes a bit of practise, but definitely pays off!

hunt out some cute graph paper notebooks

I used these MT branded tapes

perfect for making birthday or anniversary tags

Washi tape alphabet

buy or rule your own graph paper with the same width as the washi tape

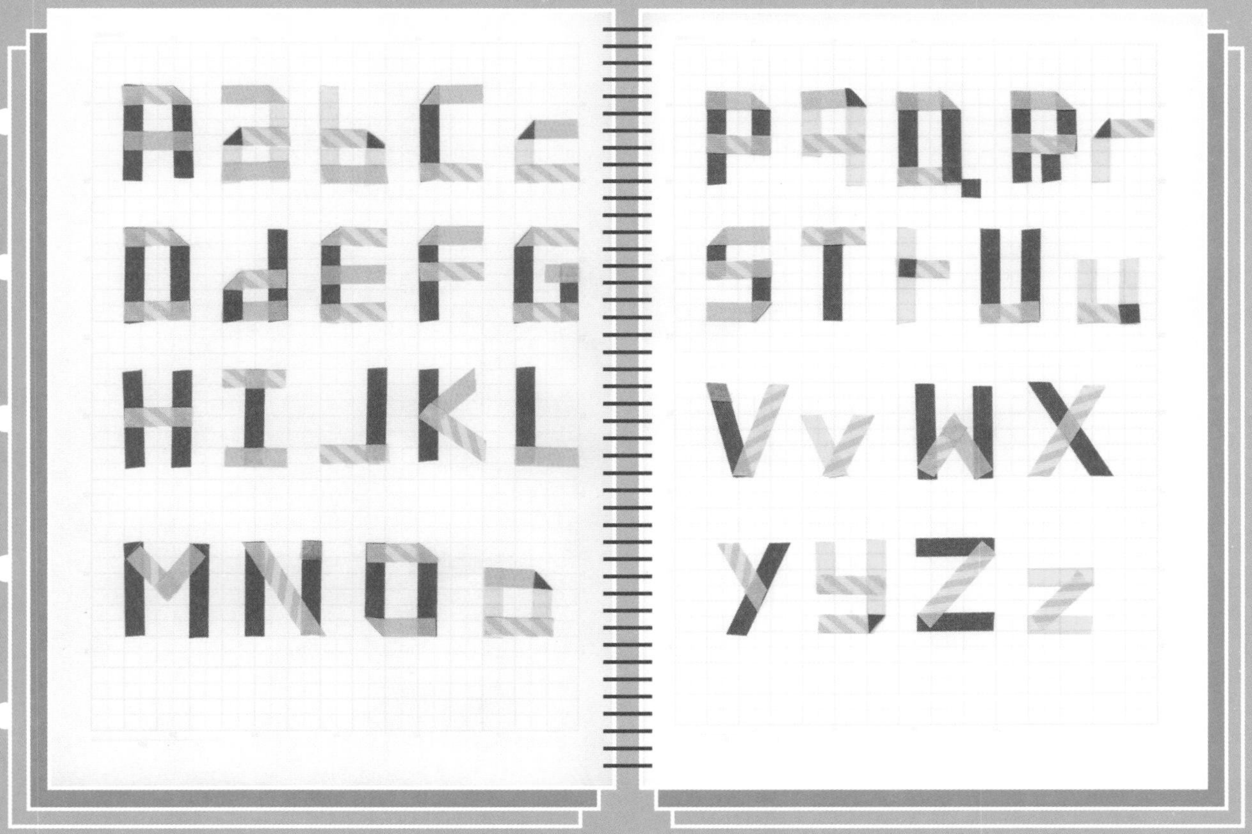

A a b C c
D d E F G
H I J K L
M N O o

P q q R r
S T F U u
V v W X
Y y Z z

I've used navy for the vertical strokes and greens for the horizontal ones

I've added a pop of yellow to some of the letters for an extra layer

Half the fun of care packages comes from the making and decoration of the box and its contents. There are lots of different creative decisions to be made, so sit down, have a cup of tea and sketch out your designs first – a good idea for any creative endeavour! Choose a theme and a colour combination, then make a list of the materials you think you'll need. Make sure your box is big (or small) and strong enough for its contents, and ensure you have all of the appropriate packing materials if you are sending your box through the mail. The following pages are designed to spark your imagination and introduce you to a range of techniques that will help you style your care package to suit your loved one.

THIS WAY UP

Thinking outside the box

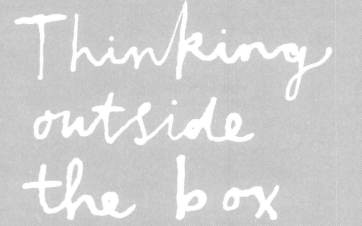

Equipment

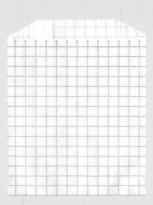

You'll need a bit of a care package tool box to make many of the things on these pages. If you have pinking shears, tapes, glue, scissors, a scalpel, pens and a cutting mat, you're in a good place to start!

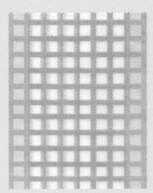

pins and needles

THINGS TO CUT WITH

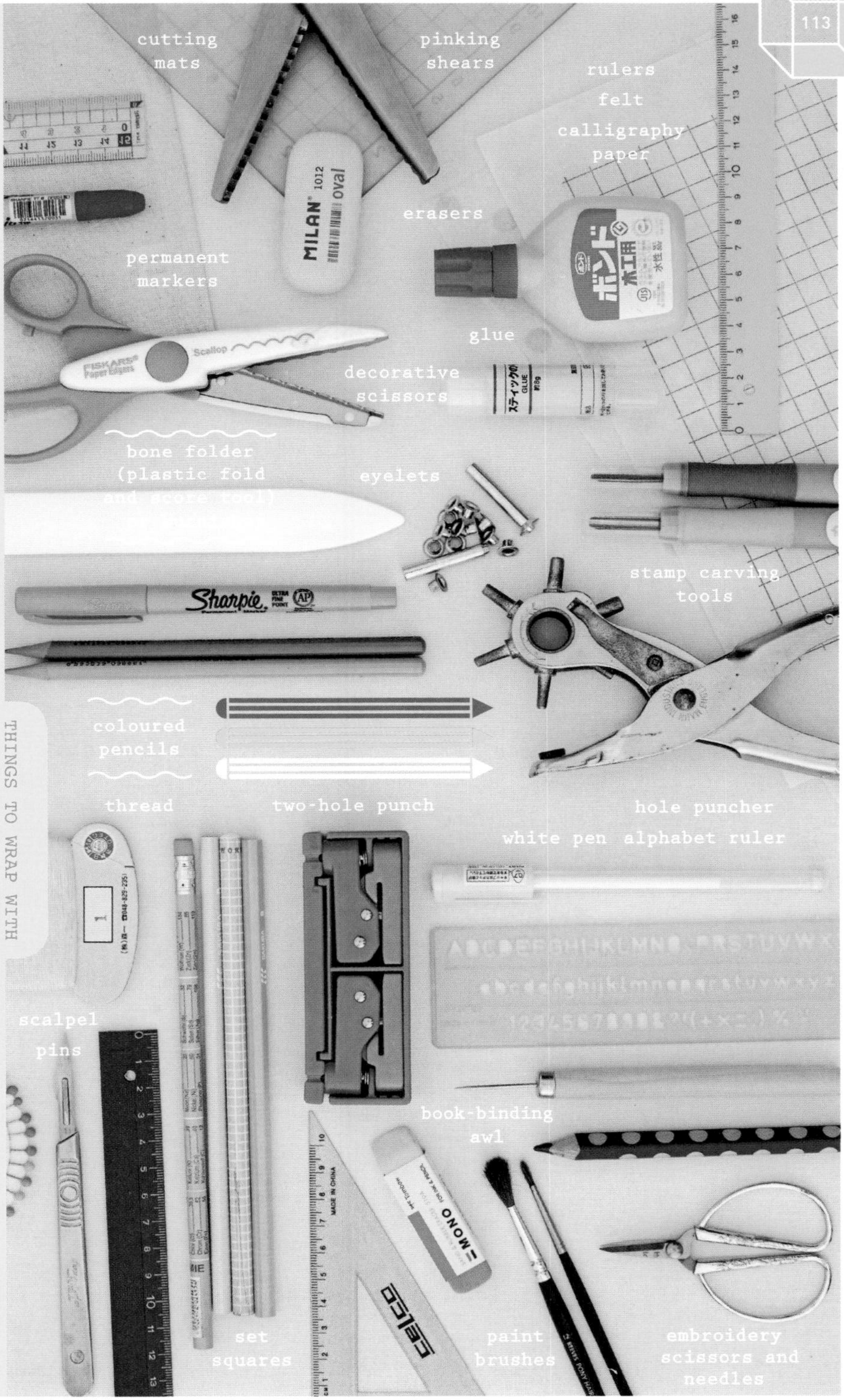

THINGS TO CRAFT WITH

THINGS TO WRITE WITH

THINGS TO WRAP WITH

cutting mats

pinking shears

rulers
felt
calligraphy
paper

erasers

permanent markers

glue

decorative scissors

bone folder
(plastic fold
and score tool)

eyelets

stamp carving
tools

coloured pencils

thread

two-hole punch

hole puncher
white pen alphabet ruler

scalpel
pins

book-binding
awl

set
squares

paint
brushes

embroidery
scissors and
needles

Colour palette ideas

When I start planning a care package, the first thing I do is think about the key item I'll be including, then build a colour palette around it. For instance, if it's a mother and baby pack and I've made a pastel-coloured softy, it will influence the other things I make or buy. Here are some of my favourite palettes to use as a starting point for your creativity.

Food and fiction writer, traveller, obsessive coffee drinker and British Shorthair owner Melbourne, Australia

Linda and I have been friends since the early 1990s and we've travelled together a lot since then, but back in the early days, if one of us was going away, we would make each other a care package that you weren't allowed to open until you were seated on the plane.

This was largely in the pre-Internet, pre-smartphone and pre-crazy-airport-security-buzzkill days, so there was no worrying about what you could and couldn't carry, and you weren't able to order exotic things from dream cities online, so travel was a genuinely new and exciting experience.

The packages – generally bulging envelopes covered in quotes and stickers – usually consisted of a letter, a mix tape, some chocolate, maybe some cigarettes and a little bottle of gin. (It really was a different time ...)

We were both massive fans of *Friends* back then and would watch it together every Monday night, and one mix tape she made me had snatches of *Friends* dialogue between tracks. She went to work in the US for a few months, so we'd still send letters and parcels of random things: she sent me Betsey Johnson socks and Chick-Fil-A

wrappers; I sent her copies of the local music street press, lip gloss and logoed napkins from favourite cafes. These days, a travel care package would be something similar (minus the cigarettes and gin) but slightly less low-rent – perhaps a USB of music or TV, a facial spray to stop you drying out on the flight, some chocolate-coated marzipan and a letter.

These packages are best delivered at the drop-off point after the airport run, which I think is the most essential part of the travel care package. It's important to send people off in style.

make your own
mix CD origami
cover
(page 62)

make a black-and-
white rock-and-
roll mix tape
care package

draw a design
onto your CD
with a
permanent marker

FOR JANE

clash up black-
and-white
patterns

Susan handmade the
black-and-white
cup and buttons

black and white,
rock and roll,
timeless and unisex

Boxes

MAKE YOUR OWN BOX

If you have the time and patience, making your own box allows you the most creativity; you can personalise every part of your package, both inside and out.

On pages 233–237, you will find a number of templates ready to be photocopied and transferred to the paper or card of your choice, but you can dismantle any box you like and create your own template by tracing its edges and marking the folds.

Before you choose the paper or card to make your box from, think about what you will be including in your package, as the box needs to be sturdy enough to accommodate the contents. You might need to practise constructing your box from a few different thicknesses of paper or

card to make sure your box will be appropriately strong; if you're worried about waste, you can always test your materials by building small, rather than full-size, versions of your box. Then you can use these for another care package project!

If you want to go the extra mile with your custom-built box, you can line it with fun coloured or patterned paper, or even washi tape. Just make sure that you line the inside of the box before you assemble it, while it is still flat, as it's much easier to do it this way.

Remember, the heavier the card or paper stock you use, the firmer you'll need to be with your folds. Scoring along the folded edges with the back of your scalpel or craft knife, or with a proper paper scorer or folding bone, is the best way to get lovely crisp folds and a neat finish.

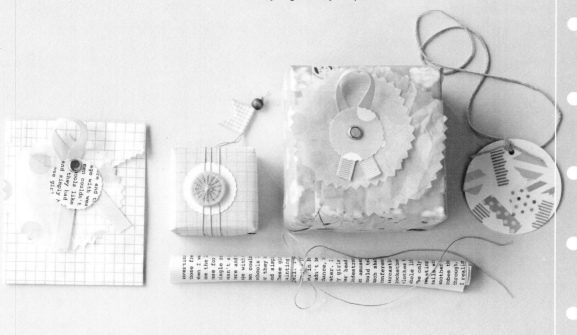

Boxes

STORE-BOUGHT ALTERNATIVES

There are quite a few wonderful boxes to be found at craft stores, office supply stores, post offices, online gift stores and all sorts of unexpected places – I found some wonderful, inexpensive polka-dot boxes at a shop in my local Chinatown. You can always rely on the office supply store for perfectly practical kraft boxes just waiting for a makeover, but I also recommend looking for storage or media boxes; you may be surprised by what you find.

PRETTY UP A BROWN KRAFT BOX

With a natural kraft base, try...

using a simple, elegant palette of white or black

cutting up vintage magazines and making collages

using just one super-bright colour, like yellow, pink, red or aqua

covering your box with vintage stamps

using a bright ribbon and name tag

tying with natural string and attaching an origami heart (page 78) or fresh flowers, leaves or branches (if your box is hand-delivered)

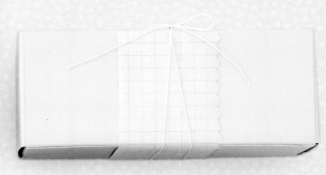

Boxes

wrap tiny
boxes with
love and
care

mix up box
sizes and
shapes

egg carton
from my
favourite free-
range organic
brand

belly band
paper from my
favourite
baker

prettied up
kraft boxes
look great in
multiples

Vintage papers

I love to buy vintage papers and advertising materials when travelling or online. It's great to wrap special-occasion presents in or as a feature band around a brown paper package.

Boxes

draw faces and add tiny sticker cheeks to your free-range organic eggs

if you have chickens in your garden, fresh eggs make for a cute package

craft upcycled egg cartons with papers, twine and tags

TAKEAWAY FOOD CONTAINERS

It may seem like a funny suggestion, but takeaway food packaging has become smarter and, in some cases, more attractive over the years. Unused cardboard takeaway containers with handles – the kind you might get from your local Chinese restaurant – make a great home for care package components, and are nowadays often found in party supply stores. You can even dress up a polystyrene container with a cute paper belly-band. Don't discount the humble takeaway box; you'll find that, with a bit of love, these utilitarian containers can become super-stylish and surprisingly pretty with a few thoughtful additions.

PRE-LOVED BOXES

I'm not sure if it is because I am a graphic designer, or if it's just a thing that some people do, but I love to keep – or, dare I say it, to hoard – pretty boxes and packaging that has housed things I have bought. I've always loved hermit crabs, too, so maybe it's the idea of giving something old a new purpose, rather than throwing it away, that I appreciate.

Pre-loved boxes are wonderful for housing care packages, since you are reusing something that would otherwise be pulped or go to landfill – not to mention it won't cost you anything. Try collecting and saving shoe boxes, garment boxes, soap boxes, vintage board game boxes (if you've lost half the pieces), perfume boxes, wooden wine boxes, hat boxes, old suitcases and school cases, and any nicely shaped cardboard box that you've come across. If you have a friend who, for instance, loves to buy shoes or has expensive taste in wine but always throws out the boxes, ask if she wouldn't mind passing any particularly beautiful boxes on to you. My mum is always bringing me things that she thinks I can make use of – and most of the time I can!

for maximum impact,
make sure your food
offering is textural
or colourful

air plants make
wonderful care
package additions

Jars and bottles

VINTAGE FINDS

Thrift stores are the perfect place to hunt for vintage jars and bottles. There are so many wonderful shapes and designs to scout for!

If the lids on any of the jars you find are a little corroded, you can still package non-edibles in them, disguising the rust with a piece of fabric secured with an elastic band and finished off with a pretty ribbon. Don't dismay if you are looking to package pickles, jams or spreads in vintage jars with corroded or missing lids: many vintage jars were produced in standard sizes that still exist today, and your local canning and preserving supply store may carry lids that fit.

Vintage bottles are ideal for homemade tomato sauce (see page 102) or homemade lemonade. If you brew your own beer, why not bottle it in some vintage flip-top bottles (replacement rubber seals are easy to pick up online) to finish off the 1890s artisan theme?

STORE-BOUGHT ALTERNATIVES

There is a fantastic selection of inexpensive glass jars and bottles to be found in stores, especially culinary supply stores or canning and preserving specialists, where you can choose from the largest pickling jar to the tiniest jam jar, from practical metal or plastic screw-top lids to pretty glass and cork lids.

What you fill the jar with, as well as the jar you choose, will depend on how you are delivering your package. If you are sending it via post, you should opt for plastic jars to avoid breakages. However, there is a downside to plastic jars: you can't sterilise them properly, which rules out using them for jams, preserves or pickles. If your heart is set on sending preserves in the mail, several small glass jars packaged very well with bubble wrap are much more likely to survive the post than one big one. Whether you're using plastic or glass, make sure you choose an option with a sturdy screw-top lid to avoid a spilling or spoiling disaster!

Packaging food

pastels, spots, grids, natural fabric and twine make for a pretty offering

vegan banana and apple loaf recipe page 90

glue vintage papers onto your bags

make origami hearts (page 78)

make your own tags

washi tape the outside of your box

wrap store-bought chocolate in baking paper

make a tag to match your bag

decorate the inside of your box

line with cute wax paper

wrap sweets in a tube

this is an upcycled see through box

HOME MADE

HOME MADE

HOME MADE

Tins

I still have a tin that was given to me when I was a little girl. I had felt left out at a family party, where most of the kids were a little older than me. A family friend, Brian, went and bought me a tin of Mackintosh chocolates so I could share with the group. In no time, I had forgotten my worries and was happily playing along with the rest of the kids. Looking back, I realise this was one of my first care package experiences. Brian's act of kindness really resonated with me, hence why I still have the tin to this day. It may look vintage now, but originally it was bright, shiny and new, a segue to happiness.

VINTAGE FINDS

I love to collect vintage tins. I am always on the lookout for them online or at flea markets, and I especially love mid-century designs. Old tins may not be appropriate to house edible goods, but are fantastic for just about anything else: a DIY first-aid kit, sewing items, paper-crafting supplies, photographs, fabric or children's toys.

STORE-BOUGHT ALTERNATIVES

I've been known to buy items I will never use just for the tin. Toffee tins and tea and biscuit tins are the best for storing my ever-growing ephemera collection! A store-bought tin is great for packaging homemade sweet treats and baked goods – I find they really hold the freshness in. If you are lucky enough to find a great-looking new tin, with a design you love, why not buy a couple? Keep one for yourself and use the other for your next care package.

try using
cute drink
cans as vases

always choose
biodegradable
bubble wrap

gold
handles and
cute design,
just perfect
for a
makeover

beautiful
natural rope
handles

Bags

CALICO BAGS

Fabric bags are great for packaging goods, especially if you are including food in your parcel. A fresh baguette popping out of the top of a fabric-stamped calico bag is an adorable sight! You can tie the handles together with a ribbon or sew a button onto the front and loop some twine onto the back, or add a bright fabric pocket to the front to carry your handwritten letter. If you have an old shirt that you are going to dissect for scraps, unpick the pocket and add it to your bag.

You can liven up a plain calico bag by stamping a bold repetitive pattern all over (see page 68 for inspiration). Make sure you use fabric stamp pads, and wash your stamped bag before using (especially if you are including food in your package). You are also gifting a reusable item to your loved one, so think of their personality, aesthetic and favourite colours before adding your pocket or fabric stamping. See pages 66–69 for more on how to stamp, including design ideas and templates.

UPCYCLED BAGS

I am a bit of a hoarder when it comes to well-designed retail bags. I have a large collection at home, made up mostly of interesting bags from overseas holidays and my favourite local deli and provisions stores. If a bag is made out of beautiful paper, has cute handles or an interesting design, I like to personalise it and turn it into a brand new version of itself. Buttons, washi tape, a bit of watercolour, stitched fabric or anything else that takes my fancy may be added to the original design. I love to use these bags to house care packages. You can decorate a bag from a store your loved one frequents or give them a bag they have never seen before with embellishments that suit their style. And it's great for the environment!

MAKING A SUSTAINABLE BUBBLE WRAP BAG

If you really need to wrap your package contents with care, you can buy wonderful biodegradable bubble wrap from office supply stores. With a little ingenuity, you can create a cute pouch or drawstring bag to house the precious item. Thank goodness for green technology!

Bags

PAPER

I love to collect vintage Japanese packaging; whenever I am in Tokyo, my friend Shoko takes me to stores that have special sections for packaging from the Showa Era – my favourite period for packaging design. Whenever I'm in Japan, I like to indulge in my habit of collecting shopping bags. Even if I am given a simple white or one-colour bag, I'll snip off the handles and replace them with ribbons, or make my own paper handles, then add tags or stickers over the shop logo or otherwise decorate the bag in a way that gives it a whole new lease on life.

I am also a huge fan of wax-paper bags; I just think they are so beautiful. Kitchen bags, sweet bags, polka-dot plastic bags: all make wonderful packaging for the contents of your care package. Everyday things can be made extraordinary with a little bit of ingenious thinking.

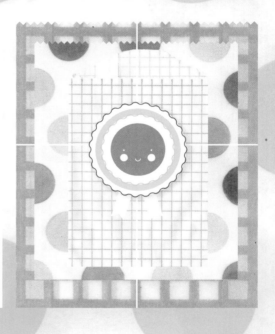

Origami

THE JAPANESE ART OF PAPER FOLDING
The art of origami can be traced back to the early years of Japan's Edo period (1603–1868). Origami models can be beautifully simple or very complex, and are often made to be given to friends and family, as well as being used to beautify parcels. Many origami items start from a square paper base; for visual effect, many papers have a two-sided design. Origami paper is usually sold in inexpensive packs of 20 or more, and is available in art and craft stores.

If you find yourself with a rainy day to while away, I highly recommend spending some time learning a few paper-folding techniques. I have included several in the pages of this book, but the internet is a treasure trove of tutorials.

Origami items are a lovely addition to the top of a hand-delivered care package, or a charming surprise tucked inside a posted one (see heart origami, page 78), but you can also go all out and make a box out of origami (see opposite), too. If you are gifting money in your care package, folding the bills into shapes is a cute way to display your offering.

The biggest tip to origami success is to take your time and fold your corners perfectly. Look into buying a bone folder if you want your folds to be extra-crisp. Origami models look extremely impressive for a minimal amount of work, especially once you have mastered the basic techniques and shapes. You will not regret making origami for your care package – in fact, you'll want to add a piece to every future package you make.

this would be great to add to a child's hospital pack

have a look at an online tutorial if you need a little extra help

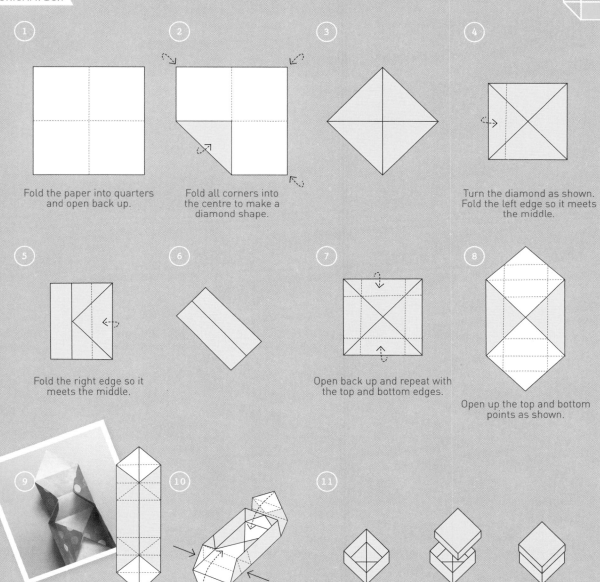

1 Fold the paper into quarters and open back up.

2 Fold all corners into the centre to make a diamond shape.

3 Turn the diamond as shown. Fold the left edge so it meets the middle.

4

5 Fold the right edge so it meets the middle.

6

7 Open back up and repeat with the top and bottom edges.

8 Open up the top and bottom points as shown.

9 Fold the left and right edges along the crease so they form the first two walls of the box.

10 Pinch and fold the creases shown and bring up the remaining two walls. Fold the remaining paper into the bottom of the box.

11 Congratulations, the body of the box is made! To make the box lid, follow the same instructions, but make the top a little bigger and the walls a little shorter. To do this, once you reach step 4, place the body of the box in the centre of the lid paper and fold the edges around the box. This way, you know the lid walls will fall outside the box body walls, as the lid top will be larger.

Wrapping

FUROSHIKI: SQUARE FABRIC WRAPPING

Furoshiki are a special kind of cloth used to wrap items in Japan. Traditionally, furoshiki were used to wrap and transport clothing and produce, but in more recent times they have been used to decorate gifts. Japanese stores sell inexpensive and beautifully designed square cloths to wrap a multitude of things.

Furoshiki can be used to wrap parts of your care package or the whole thing. Thanks to the flexible nature of the cloth, you can wrap just about any shape or size, so long as you select a fabric square big enough to wrap your parcel. Books look beautiful wrapped in furoshiki (see page 145), and a simple picnic lunch bento is ideal for wrapping furoshiki-style.

My favourite way to use furoshiki is for a chemotherapy care package (see page 182), as you can choose a beautiful scarf for your loved one to wear during treatment and have it double as wrapping for the complete package.

TENUGUI: RECTANGULAR FABRIC WRAPPING

A tenugui is a long piece of cotton cloth (around 35 cm x 90 cm or 14 in x 35½ in in size) that is traditionally used in Japan as a headband, as a souvenir, or to wrap bottles and other long gifts. I buy tenugui to use as table runners and to beautify surfaces, as there are always so many beautiful patterns to choose from. Sake or wine looks beautiful wrapped in tenugui (see page 144), and is a perfect addition to a care package as the beautiful cloth can be reused or repurposed.

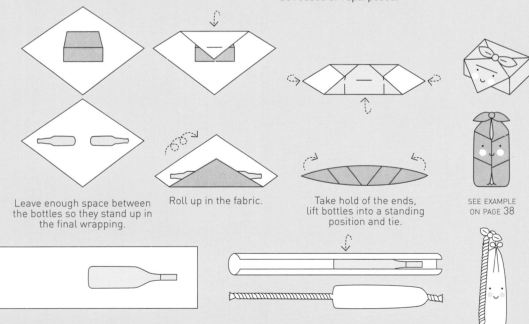

Leave enough space between the bottles so they stand up in the final wrapping.

Roll up in the fabric.

Take hold of the ends, lift bottles into a standing position and tie.

SEE EXAMPLE ON PAGE 38

Lay the bottle on the tenugui.

Roll the bottle up in the fabric, twist the ends tight and tie at the top.

SEE EXAMPLE ON PAGE 144

add your
loved one's
name

many
furoshiki
cloths are
reversible

Wrapping

add some
fabric cut
with pinking
shears

this is a
perfect way
to wrap books

Wrapping

EVERYDAY PAPER ITEMS

Don't stress if you haven't had time to make or nip out and buy wrapping paper. Newspapers, flyers, magazines, vintage papers, sheet music, pages from old books, maps, train timetables, vintage sewing patterns and just about any other kind of paper item, new or used, can be used to wrap items for your care package. Try using a colour base and putting a band of unusual paper around the middle, then fastening with string.

COLOUR BLOCKING

Bold colours can make a huge impact! Try wrapping your parcel with one bright colour, then rewrap a portion of the parcel in another colour and tie it all together with a wide coloured ribbon. I think that two brights and a pastel can look lovely together, or two brights and a metallic copper, gold or bronze. Why not use black or white as a base and bring one colour in on a diagonal? Play with shapes and lines; work squares, rectangles or triangles into your design. Try extending the colour scheme to the contents of your package for a truly integrated look.

STAMP YOUR OWN PAPER OR FABRIC

Stamping paper and fabric is a fun activity you can involve kids in, and is perfect for a crafternoon with friends. Carve your own rubber stamps or have some made from my templates (see page 69) for some truly personalised wrapping paper or fabric wrap.

Simple designs work best, and if you have a few pretty ink colours, you can layer the design. Triangles and circles work well, as you can haphazardly place them over each other to create an interconnecting design. If you are stamping onto fabric, it's important to remember to buy fabric-specific ink and to wash your fabric before use (especially if you are wrapping food).

Before stamping your final fabric or paper, have a good play. Try some ink combinations that are a little out of the ordinary (or your comfort zone). Sometimes the imperfect or the unexpected becomes your favourite design, so don't be too precious about your placements!

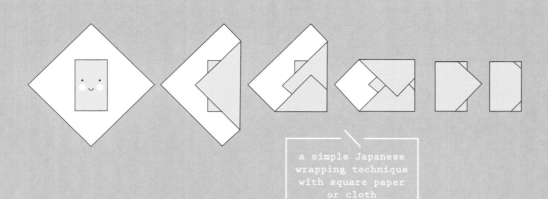

a simple Japanese wrapping technique with square paper or cloth

use your special paper to wrap as a belly band (or 'obi sash') around your parcel - not only does it look pretty, but it also means you can use your special paper on more packages

wrap items individually and tie together with string

pretty up brown paper wrapping with feathers, buttons and dried flowers

Wrapping

MAKE THE INSIDE COUNT
Think about how you are going to pad your parcel, especially if you are sending it by mail or if you are sending delicate items. Shredded paper can be functional and pretty, and you can buy biodegradable bubble wrap for those extra-precious additions.

Washi taping or collaging the interior of the box can add an extra layer of wonder when your loved one opens his or her parcel (see travel package, page 177; paper balloon box, page 200; and new love package, page 174).

Whatever you choose to do, as long as any precious items are properly wrapped, you can go wild and craft up an interior storm.

use washi tapes in
different thicknesses

I love shredding
bright paper,
kraft paper and
newspaper

Tags and decorating

don't forget to have fun!

clash up colours and patterns

bright coloured bags look fantastic together

a perfect crafternoon project!

give your tiny bags handles and fasten with stamps

add stitching
to the back of
a coaster

try
animal
shapes

use
vintage-
looking
pins to
attach
tags

Care
Package

Coffee
& T.V.

use coffee
filters for
labels

make
a post-
modern
rosette

make
hearts
out
of maps

try
different
shapes and
sizes

tiny
envelopes
make cute
tags

add
buttons
and
stamps

NUMBER ONE HUMAN

rubber
stamp onto
fabric

Making labels

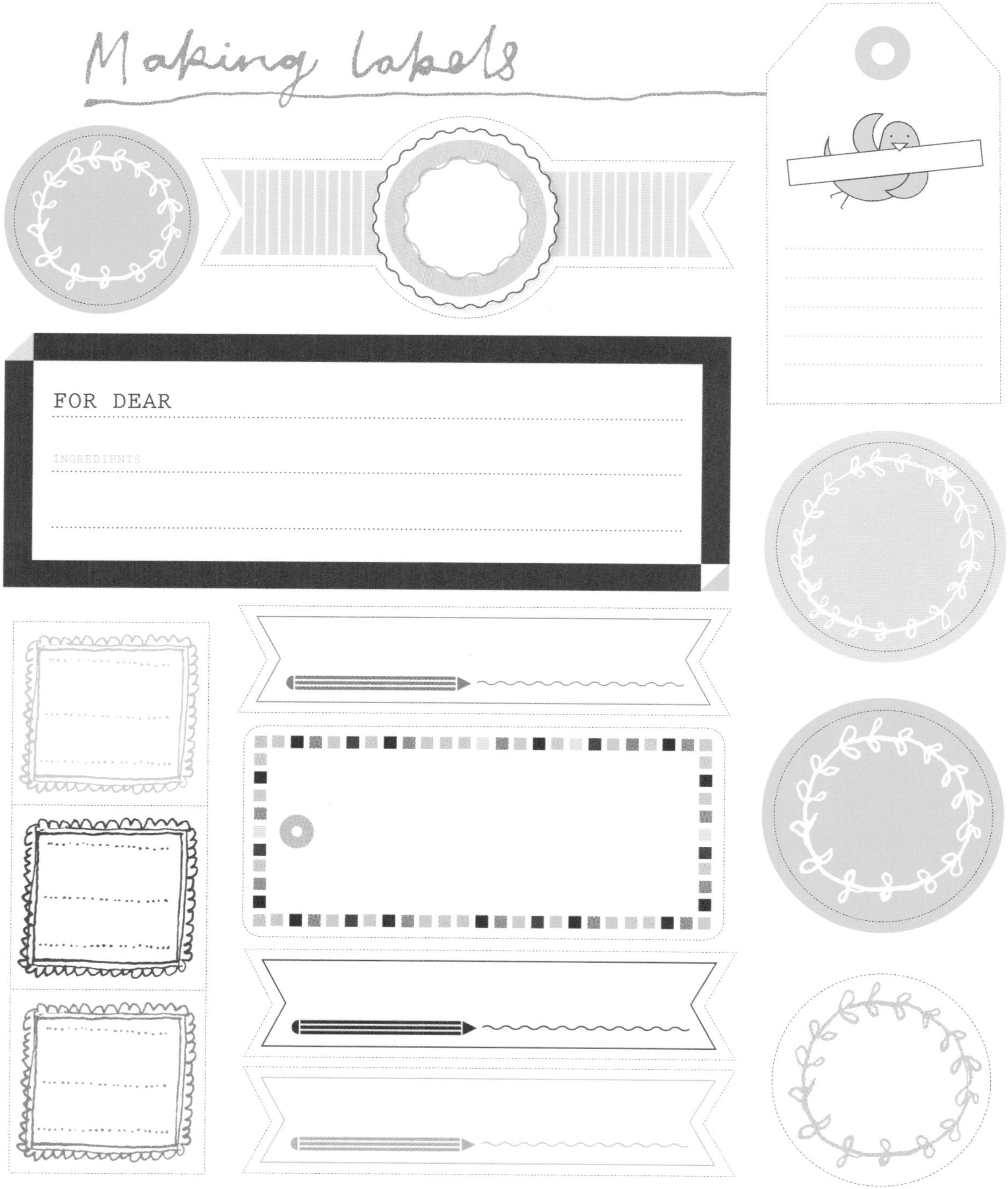

FOR DEAR

INGREDIENTS

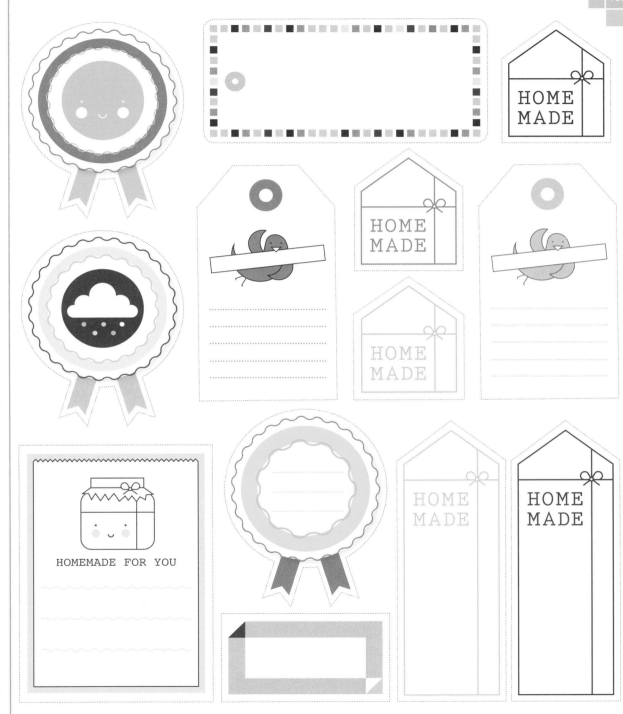

HOME
MADE

HOME
MADE

HOME
MADE

HOMEMADE FOR YOU

HOME
MADE

HOME
MADE

Care packages are infinitely customisable for just about any person or occasion – but the sheer number of possibilities can be a little overwhelming! Do you make something simple and from the heart, or do you opt for the over-the-top, super-charming option? How the care package will be delivered, the reason you are sending it, how much time you have, and the kind of person your recipient is will all contribute to the kind of care package you make. Don't let yourself feel stressed if you're working with a tiny budget or scant free time. Limitations often give rise to our greatest creative moments!

In this chapter, you'll find a list of my favourite care package themes to help you put together something special for your loved one. If you can't find one that's just right for the occasion, why not mix and match components? The possibilities are endless.

THIS WAY UP

The complete
package

" The humblest tasks
get beautified
if loving hands
do them. "

Louisa May Alcott, *Little Women*

Away
from
home

Living, working or studying overseas

letters from family members, friends, teachers

handmade card (see page 84)

newspaper cuttings

sweets and snacks from your country or town

a book written by a local author

local and national newspaper articles

pyjamas or cosy socks

origami photo book (page 72)

postcards or mementoes from their favourite haunts

homemade cookies (page 92)

mix tapes (see page 62)

USB filled with listenable or watchable goodies

cute personalised plastic or porcelain tea/coffee mug

mini country flag

daggy local souvenirs

make a paper plane out of a map or letter

use maps and airmail stickers to decorate the interior of your package

add your loved one's name

special delivery
GUEST PACKAGE

washi-taped box interior

card designed by Hana Akiyama; wrapping papers designed by Natsuko Kozue and Yumi Kitagishi

和三盆糖入
小倉汁

beautifully wrapped separates

the care package was hand delivered by bicycle in furoshiki cloth wrapping

HIKI KOMURA

Curator of UGUiSU shoppe, a bespoke Japanese stationery and gift store Tokyo, Japan

I studied in Australia for one year as an exchange student when I was fifteen, and also later for a few years, living with Australian families both times.

The packages my mum used to send me usually contained things that I missed from home, which were not so easy to get in Australia back in the late 90s: tea, Japanese mayonnaise, rice crackers, CDs, books to read and teenagers' magazines. She also included Pocky or other sweets to give to the kids in the family I was staying with.

I always looked forward to these packages from Mum; each time one arrived I'd get so excited. But once I opened the parcel, it always made me miss home more, and I'd cry reading the letter included in it. My mum packed those packages hoping they would make me feel closer to home and feel less homesick, but it was a bit hard – especially during the first year away from home!

When I make care packages to send to my dear friend Michelle in Australia, they include some tea and hokkario hot packs that will keep her warm in the cold Melbourne winter; beautifully packaged little things or paper items that remind me of her, which I find and collect; and a small amount of the Japanese incense I like at the time, so that when she opens the package she can smell a bit of Japan.

Armed forces

- for guys: razors, aftershave balm
- for girls: cleanser, tinted moisturiser
- handmade card (see page 84)
- letters from kids, family and friends
- origami photo book (page 72)
- handmade journal (page 50) and pens
- USB filled with podcasts
- CDs or DVDs
- mix tape (see page 62)
- quality cotton underwear
- cosy socks
- beanie
- sunglasses
- SPF face moisturiser and body sunscreen
- toiletries, hand and foot creams
- good-quality comb
- a cheery or witty book

- playing cards, Uno, travel-size Scrabble or other board games
- newspaper cuttings and magazines
- crossword and sudoku books
- colouring books and pencils
- homemade cookies (page 92) or other treats
- homemade soap (page 76)
- favourite snacks
- instant noodles
- condiments
- instant coffee, hot chocolate, tea bags or homemade tea bags (page 82)
- muesli or energy bars
- favourite lollies, sweets and candy
- chewing gum
- disposable hand-warmers for winter

homemade chocolate is wrapped in wood-patterned paper

buy an alphabet stamp set and personalise items

creatively wrap your letter - this envelope is handmade

choose a USB to suit your loved one's personality

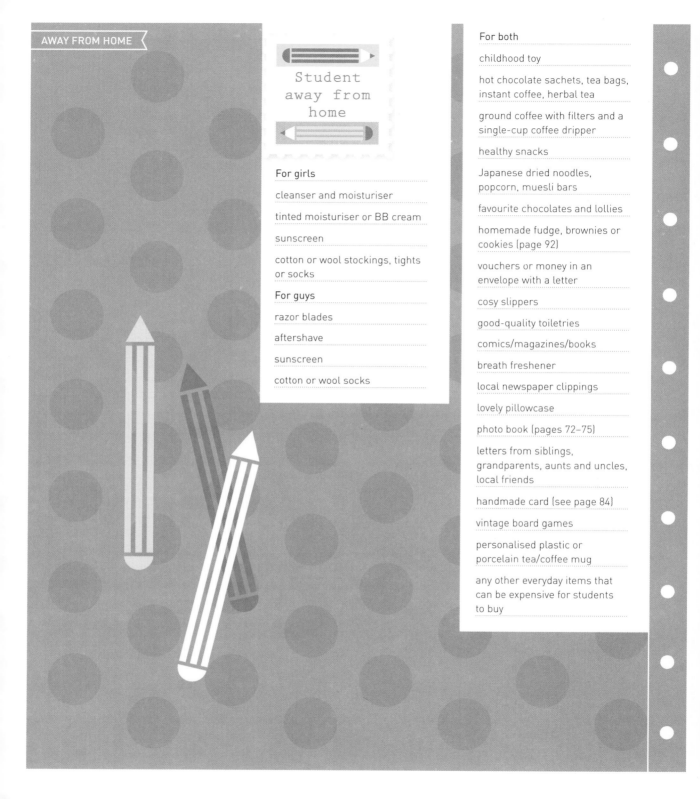

Student away from home

For girls

cleanser and moisturiser

tinted moisturiser or BB cream

sunscreen

cotton or wool stockings, tights or socks

For guys

razor blades

aftershave

sunscreen

cotton or wool socks

For both

childhood toy

hot chocolate sachets, tea bags, instant coffee, herbal tea

ground coffee with filters and a single-cup coffee dripper

healthy snacks

Japanese dried noodles, popcorn, muesli bars

favourite chocolates and lollies

homemade fudge, brownies or cookies (page 92)

vouchers or money in an envelope with a letter

cosy slippers

good-quality toiletries

comics/magazines/books

breath freshener

local newspaper clippings

lovely pillowcase

photo book (pages 72–75)

letters from siblings, grandparents, aunts and uncles, local friends

handmade card (see page 84)

vintage board games

personalised plastic or porcelain tea/coffee mug

any other everyday items that can be expensive for students to buy

include a childhood toy in your package

decorate your box inside and out

MARGARET HAAS

Stationer and crazy cat lady Los Angeles, USA

Leaving home for college is a rite of passage in the States, and probably the biggest one that I've ever experienced. When I left for university in Santa Cruz it was my first time living in another city and being away from my friends and family. I was crazy excited. Though it was only a six-hour drive or a quick plane ride away from home, I was also sad to be separated from my family and the boyfriend who would eventually become my husband.

Care packages sent and received kept me near to those I couldn't see. The best away-from-home care packages remind the recipient of the place she left and provide a connection that can only come through the mail. Familiar sights and tastes instantly transport us back home.

Mom's care packages to me were always filled with essentials that I had forgotten to buy: aspirin, batteries and printer ink were all valuable, but thoughtful, too. She never forgot to include snacks from the pantry that I constantly craved as a child, such as yoghurt-covered pretzels, peanut M&Ms, gummy bears, mini Snickers and circus animal cookies. I would break the seal on a care package; the scent of sweets from my childhood would rise from the box; and I would be transported 400 miles south to my home.

To get, you must give; mail karma is a real thing. So I began to make surprise packages for my friends and family back home as well as for loved ones around the world. A handwritten letter was the cornerstone for each bundle I sent, but I knew they wouldn't be complete unless accompanied by objects connected to my new life. All of my care packages contained the same elements but were wildly different, depending on the recipient. Each featured something sweet, a photograph or drawing, and a souvenir or trinket, all wrapped up in a decorated box – usually covered in stickers.

No package was more thought out than the one I would send to my beau for Valentine's Day. A chocolate banana slug from the local sweet shop Marini's was a must. (UC Santa Cruz's mascot is a banana slug; it is meant to poke fun at the fierce athletic competitiveness for which American colleges are known.) Other treats of all kinds were included in the overly decorated parcel: a photo of a place that we would go on his next visit, a coupon for a romantic night on the town and, of course, a long, handwritten love letter. The parcels I sent and received during college kindled a lifelong love affair with care packages. I have never stopped sending them. These days, when I receive one, it still gives me a sense of a place that I've never visited in a way that no email or phone call ever could.

Family,
love and
friendship

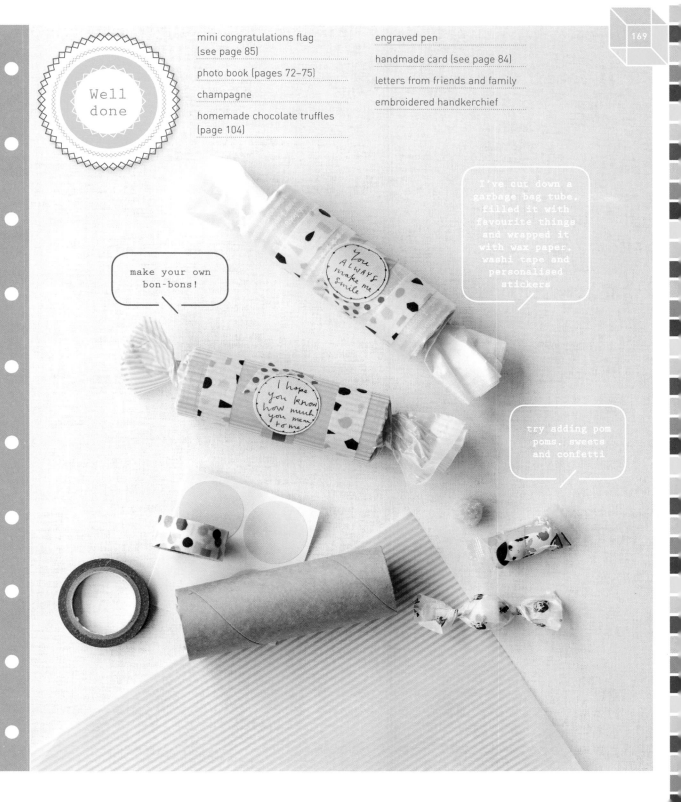

Well done

mini congratulations flag
(see page 85)

photo book (pages 72–75)

champagne

homemade chocolate truffles
(page 104)

engraved pen

handmade card (see page 84)

letters from friends and family

embroidered handkerchief

make your own
bon-bons!

You ALWAYS make me smile

I hope you know how much you mean to me

I've cut down a
garbage bag tube,
filled it with
favourite things
and wrapped it
with wax paper,
washi tape and
personalised
stickers

try adding pom
poms, sweets
and confetti

New
mother
and
baby

For mother

dry shampoo

cleanser and tinted moisturiser

lip balm

good-quality shampoo and
conditioner

cosy socks

a book on a topic she loves

a new towel

homemade food, like muesli
(page 98), tomato sauce for
pasta (page 102), or dishes that
can be popped in the freezer

lovely versions of long-life
pantry items, including coffee
and tea, dried fruits and nuts,
pasta, rice and other grains

a favourite cheese and biscuits

handmade journal (page 50)

personalised plastic or
porcelain tea/coffee mug

For baby

nappies (diapers) or nappy
washing service

baby lotions, wipes, massage oils

handmade soap (page 76)

soothing essential oils to burn,
like lavender and chamomile

soft hand towels

crochet booties

polaroid relationship book
(see pages 72–75)

origami mobile (pages 78–81)

handmade toys

rubber ducky

mini handmade quilt

make and buy
to a colour
theme (I love
natural and pink)

include handmade
tea bags and
photo book
(pages 82 and 72-75)

personalise
a toy with the
new arrival's
name

hand-make
individual tags

turn your mail satchel into a cute shoulder bag with a pretty ribbon

use naive stitching to style your mini care pack

hand-stitch a rainbow (template page 229) onto a handkerchief

New
love

handmade card (see page 84)

champagne

cute underwear

chocolates

photo book (pages 72–75)

movies

mix tapes (see page 62)

USB filled with listenable or watchable goodies

personalised plastic or porcelain tea/coffee mug

send a box
of individual
letters

make envelopes
out of music or
movie flyers

Anniversary

handmade card (see page 84)

polaroid relationship book (see pages 72–75)

champagne

handmade chocolate truffles (page 104)

voucher for a meal at your favourite restaurant

babysitter booked for a night out

embroidered handkerchief

personalised plastic or porcelain tea/coffee mug

washi-tape letters to the top of your box

wrap items individually

add a handmade photo book (page 72)

pretty up store-bought chocolate

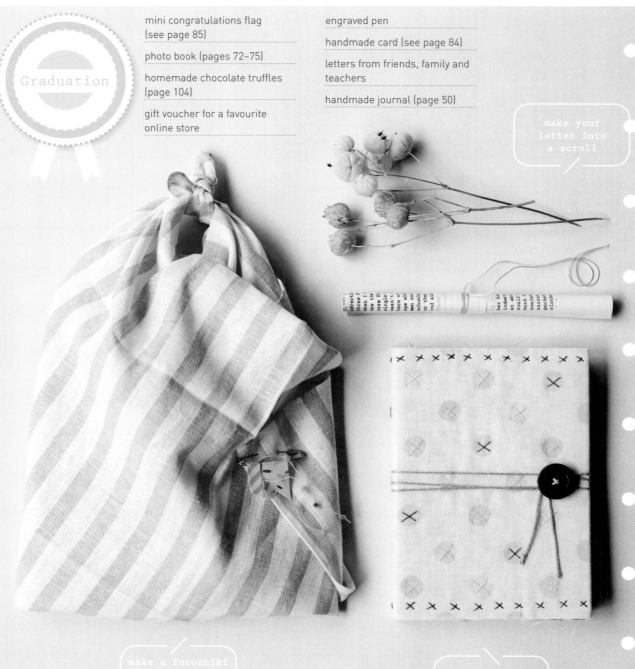

Graduation

- mini congratulations flag (see page 85)
- photo book (pages 72–75)
- homemade chocolate truffles (page 104)
- gift voucher for a favourite online store
- engraved pen
- handmade card (see page 84)
- letters from friends, family and teachers
- handmade journal (page 50)

make your letter into a scroll

make a furoshiki bag out of a handkerchief or scarf (page 230)

hand-stitched journal (page 60)

Travel

handmade card (see page 84)

Japanese individual face masks

fabric eye mask and ear plugs

mini toiletries

pocket colouring book and
good-quality mini pencils

handmade journal (page 50)

USB filled with listenable or
watchable goodies

mix tapes

a card with $10–$50 of the local
currency enclosed

travel Scrabble or Uno

mini bottle of booze

write something
meaningful

this mini care
package can be
taken on a plane
or popped in an
overnight bag

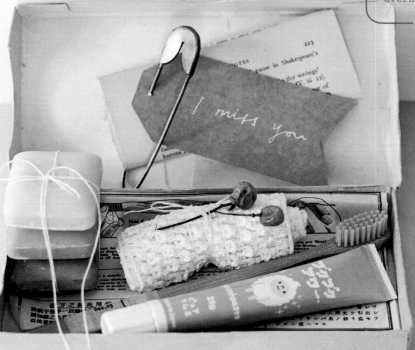

I miss you

packaged in a
vintage box

Difficult times

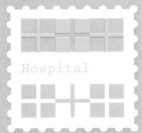

Hospital

loungewear – many stores now stock a kind of pyjama–tracksuit hybrid. I am a big fan of this hybrid, as I am not a tracksuit wearer.

crazy, happy pyjamas – giant polka-dots or another fun pattern may help cheer your loved one up

toiletries – mini cleanser, moisturiser, deodorant, toothpaste, lip balm, soap and soap container, breath freshener

dry shampoo – my number-one pick for a hospital care package, this makes keeping long hair clean much easier when showering is difficult

ear plugs and sleeping mask

cotton underwear

cosy socks or slippers

handmade card (see page 84)

a USB or their laptop filled with games and listenable or watchable goodies

magazines, books, crosswords, sudoku, mind games

photo book (pages 72–75)

hand-stitched handkerchief

fresh fruit of the patient's choice (grapes or mandarins are good)

dry biscuits

mints, barley sugar or favourite sweets

ask if your loved one …

needs laundry or housework done

has any food requests

wants you to bring anything in

wants you to organise something to do with work, friends or family

For girls:
tinted moisturiser or BB cream
bandeau bra with no straps (so if she is hooked up to an IV she can easily take it on and off) or a singlet with a built-in bra

For guys:
moisturiser,
razors,
aftershave,
good-quality comb

a natural
drawstring bag
is a lovely way to
house all
the products

Make your own toiletries pack

Buy some small plastic containers, fill with
your favourite products and make your own
labels. If your loved one is going through
chemo, hand sanitiser is VERY important

I like to include
some lavender
from my garden
in a face spray

for label
patterns and ideas
see pages 150-153

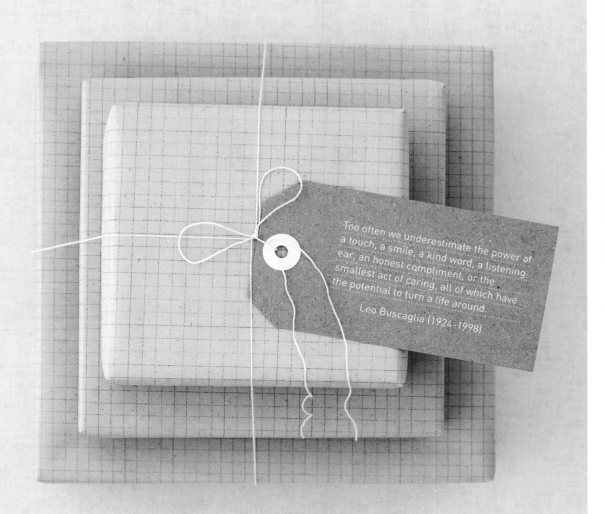

Too often we underestimate the power of a touch, a smile, a kind word, a listening ear, an honest compliment, or the smallest act of caring, all of which have the potential to turn a life around.

Leo Buscaglia (1924-1998)

Chemotherapy

handmade card (see page 84)

handmade journal (page 50)

colouring book and good-quality pencils

photo book (pages 72–75)

mints or barley sugar

cute personalised plastic teacup

fluffy socks or slippers

books and magazines

sudoku or crossword books

a fun-looking USB filled with listenable or watchable goodies

cute headphones

lip balm

hand sanitiser

soothing and anti-nausea herbal teas (chamomile, ginger and peppermint are good choices)

homemade soap (page 76)

Japanese individual face masks

homemade bath salts (page 88) and a soft toothbrush

face moisturiser or tinted moisturiser

body moisturiser

lavender essential oil for relaxation

rosehip or vitamin E oil for skin and scalp

cotton or natural fibre head scarf

fresh fruit of the patient's choice (grapes and mandarins are good)

homemade soup broth

a few varieties of dry biscuits

a cosy quilt, throw, pashmina or soft, light, warm blanket

a 'human care package' – be a good listener (see page 14)

care coupons (page 54)

furoshiki
(see page 142)
your loved one's
care package in a
bright head scarf

bamboo
toothbrushes
have lovely soft
bristles

buy small bottles
to package
toiletries and
wrap with cute
headphones

Buy a cute kitchen timer for
your loved one. Pop it on when you
visit so you don't tire them out or
overstay your welcome, leaving
space in their schedule for doctors,
nurses and other visitors.

a pineapple USB
is guaranteed to
get a smile

handmade card (see page 84)

homemade meals

lovely, easy-to-prepare food like pasta, parmesan and homemade tomato sauce (page 102)

books and magazines

puzzles and board games

terrarium in a glass jar

a 'human care package' – be a good listener, offer to drive to medical appointments and go grocery shopping (see page 14)

care coupons (page 54)

good-quality long-life pantry items from the supermarket or local deli

see also hospital care package (page 179)

Break-up

handmade card (see page 84)

a 'human care package' – be a good listener, plan nights out or trips together (see page 14)

care coupons (page 54)

a voucher for a manicure, facial or massage

individual Japanese face masks

hand-stitched handkerchief (see page 87)

vintage board game

Cultural sensitivities and bereavement

If your friend has lost a loved one and observes a specific religion, it can be a nice gesture to weave some of that religion's traditions into your care package. I've highlighted a few quick and general points below that may be helpful when you curate your package. A little bit of research will help your care package to feel sensitively made and thoughtful. Remember, though, you know your friend best - so use as many or as few of the suggestions below as you think is appropriate. At the end of the day, you want your friend to know you are there for them and thinking of them.

JUDAISM

My friend Joel told me all about the Jewish religion's mourning period known as 'sitting shiva'. If your loved one is Jewish and has lost a family member, they may observe this tradition. After your loved one has attended the funeral, they enter a seven-day mourning period. It's a time for friends and family to visit (known as a 'shiva call'), pay their respects and bring food. Mourners are not meant to cook or work among other things during this period, so it is an ideal time to make and drop off a food care package. It is considered kind and compassionate to make a home visit, but remember, if you drop the care package off in person, it may not be the right time to visit. If you are invited in, ask to help prepare the food for anyone who is hungry. Think about making and preparing food that can be shared, or including food that has a shelf- or fridge-life of a few days, and consider your friend's family's dietary requirements. Fruit baskets are popular during this period, so if you choose to make one for your loved one, consider a beautiful way to present it. A beautiful reusable basket might be a thoughtful way to package your gift, or perhaps a box with a homemade card. Chocolates, nuts and homemade biscuits also make wonderful additions.

If you are making a shiva call, avoid bringing flowers, which are not part of the Jewish mourning tradition. Some close friends and family members make a donation on behalf of the deceased to a favourite temple or charity.

BUDDHISM

Mourners traditionally wear white rather than black at a Buddhist funeral, so if you are visiting the house of a grieving friend you may consider wearing white or using white wrapping and ribbons for your care package. Candles and incense are burnt after a loved one has passed, so you may like to include either or both as a gesture in your parcel. Many Buddhists are vegetarian, so consider dietary requirements before including food in your care package.

HINDUISM

Hindu funerals are usually conducted within twenty-four hours of the deceased's passing. Until the cremation is held, no cooking is to be done in the house, so a beautifully wrapped food parcel is a wonderful way to show you care. Remember to make sure the food is vegetarian, and cooking with garlic and onion is prohibited.

ISLAM

There are two main denominations of Islam, Sunni and Shia. They have slightly different customs, so you may need to do some research before making your care package. After a burial, there are forty days of prayer gatherings in the home and a three-day mourning period, during which visitors are received. Condolences are very important: remain calm and kind, and offer hope and comfort. It is customary for friends and family to prepare and bring food. Make a food parcel, take it in person and offer to serve

RELIGIOUS
CARE PACKAGE
INCLUSIONS

a scripture quotation in beautiful calligraphy on cotton paper

incense or candles tied with a ribbon with a handwritten tag

the right colour wrapping paper for the appropriate religion

if including flowers, choose your flower colour carefully (in many cases flowers are not appropriate; see page 24)

food that has a shelf- or fridge-life of a few days and is good for sharing, such as small biscuits, small savoury items, fruit or fruitcake

it or help in any other way. Make your parcel thoughtful and include items that not only your friend but also all visitors can enjoy. Wrap it simply and dress simply as well. Decoration is seen as excessive at this time. Remember that flowers, food and money should not be present near the grave. And please be cheery, as sadness around the bereaved is not customary.

SHINTO

Shinto is the oldest religion in Japan. When a loved one passes there are over twenty rituals performed, including an intense mourning period called 'kichu-fuda', which lasts for one day. The family creates and decorates a shrine in their home, which includes a central photograph and is adorned with candles, fruits, flowers, incense and other personal items.

Friends and family traditionally give a gift of money to help reduce the financial burden. My friend Makiko told me an amount of thirty dollars is appropriate, and would be given in an envelope. If you were making a care package, a little bit of research could make your gift truly thoughtful. Find out, if you can, a favourite flower, fruit or incense, or the sort of small vase used at the shrine, and add it to your care package. Include your friend's favourite food or drink, and perhaps some of their favourite music on a decorated USB stick – or burn it to a CD and make a custom cover.

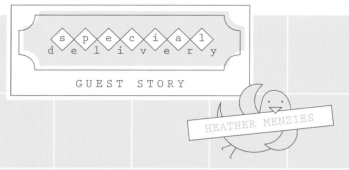

Designer, painter and illustrator Sydney, Australia

Everyone was so amazing when I was diagnosed with cancer, and continued to be amazing throughout the whole catastrophe. I received letters and cards, and I wrote to everyone and sent thank yous and hellos; it was delightful to get mail. I devoured these and still have them all in a special box.

I've always loved to read and this was my escape from chemo treatment. One of the gifts I received before I had even had surgery was *A Game of Thrones*, the first book in George R R Martin's *A Song of Ice and Fire* series, along with the whole first season of the television adaptation on an iPad. I adored it. I just withdrew into my shell on the bad days and read and watched the series. As time progressed, my partner Rich and I would walk to the bookshop down the road to buy the next book in the series; thankfully it was a long story!

I don't remember asking for anything, apart from the misery of chemo to end. I liked to have a hand rub, or my shoulders, legs or feet massaged, as the treatments made my bones ache, and people brought me hand creams, flowers, candles, faith rocks, lucky stones, a four leaf clover, scarves, wraps, food parcels, slippers and pyjamas. But above all, the gift of company was the best. I loved seeing people. They were my connection to the outside world. Even as I lost my usual energy, I never tired of laughing and hearing silly stories; I so loved to be distracted. As my world grew smaller, my friends would make sure to keep me up-to-date with everything that was happening, either visiting me at home or keeping me entertained when I went into work in between chemo treatments. When I was actually getting the chemo at the hospital, it was easier just to be by myself.

The strangest thing about the whole experience was that my favourite foods tasted awful! Breakfast cereal is my favourite food group, but nothing appealed to me while I was undergoing treatment. All food ended up tasting like pepper. So it was a delightful surprise to find that mandarins held some joy for me. I ended up liking ice cream cups from the hospital, and hot chocolate, too: Rich would make me one every afternoon as we sat in bed together and watched *Star Trek* until I fell asleep.

If I were to give someone a chemo care package, it would depend on the month. As I went through it in winter in Melbourne, the mohair wrap, warm pyjamas and handmade quilt from my sister were perfect. To me, a great chemo care package would have to include a good-quality cotton scarf (so soft and easy to wear), a good sunscreen, jojoba oil, green tea, the softest wrap or light blanket, and flowers to brighten the day. And, of course, a visit or two to cheer the recipient along their journey.

Each gift, touch, letter and moment of friendship I received made me stronger and helped me realise that chemo was just something I had to endure until it eventually passed. Those friendships and people in my life, on the other hand, are in my heart forever.

cut out fabric
squares with pinking
shears and hand-
stitch onto a
calico bag

use iron-on
adhesive on your
fabric squares
for sturdiness

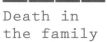

Death in the family

add roasted tomato sauce (page 102) to your package to go with the potted basil

seeds are a lovely symbol

handmade card (see page 84) or letter

hand-stitched handkerchief (see page 173)

a 'human care package' – be a good listener and an attentive friend (see page 14)

small tree to plant on behalf of the recipient's loved one

a food hamper including:

food for sharing (homemade sweet or savoury baking, cheese platter makings)

long-life pantry items (fruit and nuts, pasta, parmesan and sauce, muesli, preserves and pickles)

meals that can be frozen (lunches and dinners)

fruit, vegetables and herbs grown in your garden

Job loss

handmade card (see page 84)

lovely versions of long-life pantry items, including coffee and tea, dried fruits and nuts, pasta, rice and other grains

homemade treats such as cakes (page 90) or cookies (page 92)

homemade chocolate truffles (page 104)

a mix tape that reflects their music taste

homemade muesli (page 98), pickles or preserves

a 'human care package' – a carefree night out together, dinner at your place or an offer to babysit (see page 14)

fun movies, podcasts or books

a voucher to an online bookstore or movie/TV service

a voucher for a manicure, facial or massage

vintage board game

fruit, vegetables and herbs grown in your garden

add a touch of cheer with washi tape flags

Alice's homemade baguettes are stuffed with tomato, cheese, avocado, lettuce and basil

Just
because

Indulgence

champagne

flowers – pressed or arranged and wrapped by you

homemade bath salts (page 88)

homemade soap (page 76)

chocolate truffles (page 104)

voucher for a babysitter

movie tickets (choose Gold Class or other luxury cinema options for extra indulgence)

voucher for a facial or massage

voucher for a dinner or a show

Cosy

fluffy socks

cosy pyjamas or loungewear set

herbal tea in handmade tea bags (page 82)

homemade bath salts (page 88)

body cream

Japanese individual face masks

homemade soap (page 76)

wheat bag or hot water bottle to heat up aching muscles

vintage board game

my friend Kate knitted me these beautiful socks and sent them in a postal parcel ... just because

Relax

peonies represent prosperity, good fortune and romance

they are the twelfth wedding anniversary symbol

peonies have the most beautiful fragrance

with a permanent marker, draw a cute pattern onto picnic cups

try a simple grid design or even a woodland motif!

Italian dinner

Italian cheese, biscuits and dried figs or muscatel grapes

homemade pasta sauce (page 102)

parmesan cheese

good-quality pasta

fresh bread

mini extra-virgin olive oil

lemon curd and Italian sponge finger (savoiardi) biscuits

bottle of wine

Italian movie marathon USB

Coffee lovers

fresh beans or freshly ground coffee in a decorated bag

coffee measuring spoon

single-cup coffee dripper with filters

milk and sugar

personalised plastic, paper or porcelain tea/coffee mug or cups

homemade cookies (page 92)

To decorate the calico bag, pour a little coffee onto a plate, dip your cup rim into the coffee and carefully stamp onto the bag. I like to flick a bit of coffee over the bag when I finish my design!

Breakfast

homemade muesli (page 98)

baked fruit compote

homemade baked goods, such as scones, brioche or pastries

homemade jam

freshly squeezed juice

freshly ground coffee

herbal tea in handmade tea bags (page 82)

personalised plastic or porcelain tea/coffee mug

with a permanent marker, draw a design to match your friend's coffee preference

write your friend's name all over the coffee bag

Espresso

SHORT macchiato

FLAT white

S SHORT

CAFE latte

> "I like cappuccino, actually. But even a bad cup of coffee is better than no coffee at all."
>
> David Lynch

Time poor

care coupons (page 54)

homemade soap (page 76)

cosy socks

essential oils for stress
– choose from bergamot,
cedarwood, chamomile,
lavender, jasmine, orange
and rose

*see also breakfast or Italian dinner
packages (pages 198 and 197)*

Library

set up an old-school book
lending system

make a personalised library card

house some books you
know your loved one will adore
in a cute office storage module

replenish with new books every
week

a wonderful add-on to the
coffee- or tea-lover's packs
(pages 198 and 207)

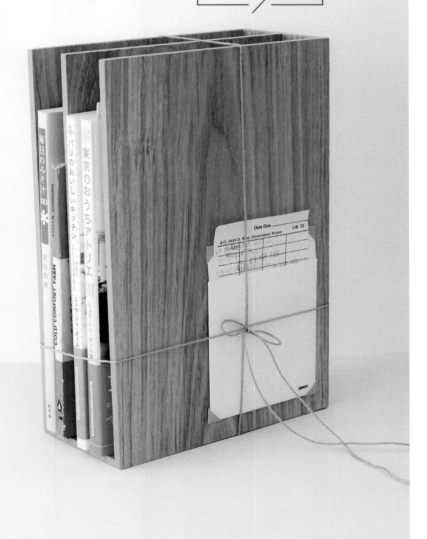

include an
unexpected book,
and a note on why
you love it

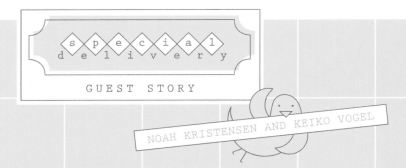

Pen pals Århus and San Francisco

During the making of *Care Packages*, I asked my friends on Instagram to send my PO Box 26 some petite parcels to be featured in the book. One of my followers, Noah, who lives in Denmark, was desperate to send a tiny package, but personal circumstances meant he would be unable to meet the postal deadline. I did message him and tell him he could have a bit longer, but he was worried his crafting skills were not up to the standard of the excellent parcels I had already received. He wanted to buy my first book, *Snail Mail*, so he could learn a few crafty things before sending something.

In the meantime, for every parcel that I received and posted to Instagram, Noah would write a wonderful positive comment praising the efforts of each creator. Even though he felt too overwhelmed to make something himself, he brought the most supportive atmosphere to the project.

Another lovely follower of mine, Keiko, who lives in San Francisco, had been encouraging Noah to make a parcel. Out of pure kindness, she bought a copy of *Snail Mail*, packaged it up beautifully with a letter and sent it to Denmark. When the postie delivered the package to Noah, he burst into happy tears! The postie said that it had made her day, and Noah sent her off with some nuts and a bottle of water. It's lovely, because *Snail Mail* ended up being the perfect care package for Noah, and Noah paid it forward with his own gesture of care to his postie.
—MM

Noah and I met on Instagram through Michelle's petite parcel project. We bonded over a shared love of kawaii, cats and snail mail, and we quickly became pen friends.

One day Noah told me he was feeling heavy-hearted and was having a tough time. I knew he was a bookworm and that he wanted *Snail Mail* badly, so I thought it would cheer him up if I sent him a copy of the book. I called my local bookstore to order it in and the lovely lady on the phone cheerfully told me that they had a copy right then and there! So I immediately hopped on my bike and went to get the book.

I had such a fun time writing a letter and making a little package to send to my new friend far away in Scandinavia. And it put a big smile on my face when Noah messaged me a week later to tell me that he had received the package and that the book had made him very happy!

I love the creative community of Instagram and have met so many talented, wonderful people thanks to *Snail Mail*.
—Keiko

Keiko is such a wonderful person. Out of nowhere, she wrote to me and asked if I had ordered *Snail Mail* yet. Sadly, I said no and she told me to send her my address. I was stunned that a complete stranger would want to do something so selfless and wonderful for me. What a gesture! Not only did she take time out of her busy day to make the effort to buy the book, but she also wrote a beautiful little letter, wrapped it all in a gorgeous tote bag and some lovely green paper, and took it to the post office to mail it out so I could get it as soon as possible.

In a world where it seems like we are getting more greedy and self-obsessed by the day, it is truly a gift to know there are still people like Keiko, who wanted to do something simply because she knew it would make me very happy. Every time I read *Snail Mail* or see it up on my bookshelf, it puts a huge smile on my face.
—Noah

FUTURE
CAT DADDY
NOAH

Noah,
Keiko and I
all love snail mailing,
cats, Japan, reading and
mid-century pottery.

Hi Noah, I am so glad to meet
you through Instagram!
I love your beautiful gallery +
it's always happy to see your
cheerful messages popping up!

Thank you so much for your
support and encouraging words.
I'm very excited about
exchanging Snail mails with you.

Although we live far away
I think we have a lot in common
love of cats + all the furry friends,
Snail mail, kawaii, make things,
eat organic, and I'm a vegetarian too.

Hope things will get better soon
and you'll enjoy ♥ Michelle's ♥ much
wonderful "Snail Mail" book as much
I did. Look foward to seeing your
creations!

Much Love,
keiko

House
party

bottle of wine

bread and cheese

pasta, parmesan and
homemade tomato sauce
(page 102)

DVDs for a movie marathon

USB or mix CD to dance to

homemade truffles (page 104)

biscuits, ice cream and other
sweet things

individual Japanese face masks

cosy socks

theme up your
care package
with snow flakes

I love naturals
and pastels
together

Winter

fluffy socks

cosy pyjamas or loungewear set

herbal tea in handmade tea
bags (page 82)

homemade bath salts (page 88)

bath accessories

candles

homemade soap (page 76)

wheat bag or hot water bottle to
heat up aching muscles

Japanese heated pocket
warmers with a cute cover

Chocolate lovers

homemade chocolate truffles
(page 104)

chocolate hearts wrapped
beautifully

white, milk and dark chocolate
treats

chocolate with different cacao
percentages

favourite chocolate bars
repackaged or relabelled

drinking chocolate and
marshmallows

personalised plastic or
porcelain tea/coffee mug

Afternoon tea

homemade chocolate truffles
(page 104)

homemade cookies (page 92)

homemade cake (page 90)

herbal tea in handmade tea
bags (page 82)

freshly ground coffee in a
decorated bag

personalised plastic or
porcelain tea/coffee mug

milk and sugar

Tea lovers

herbal tea in handmade tea
bags (page 82)

milk and sugar

personalised glass teacup or
vintage cup and saucer

homemade cookies (page 92)

with a white
pen draw a design
onto your
box and cup

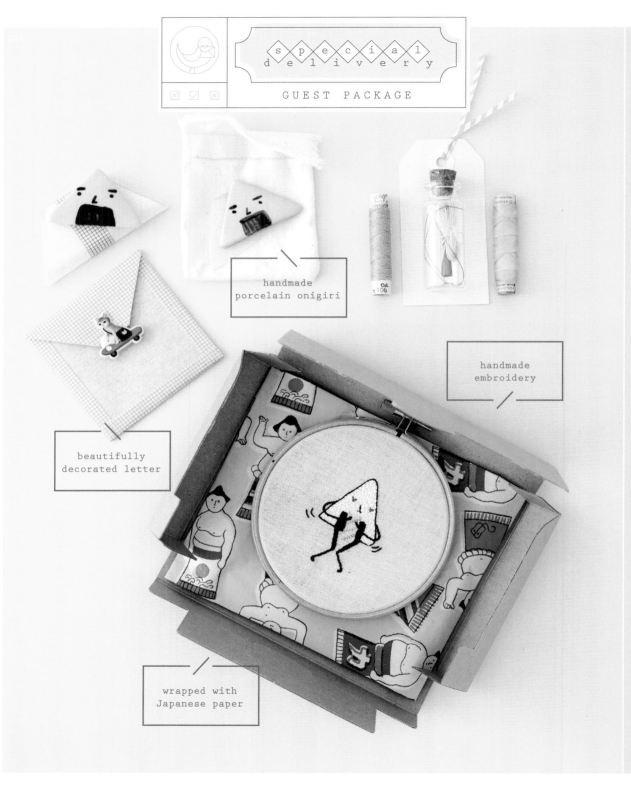

handmade
porcelain onigiri

handmade
embroidery

beautifully
decorated letter

wrapped with
Japanese paper

LAURA AMEBA

Embroidery and stitch expert, author Barcelona, Spain (and sometimes Japan)

I was born in 1986 in Santiago, Chile, and spent my teenage years writing letters to one of my best friends. We studied at different schools, so a good way to share secrets with each other was to send letters during the week; sometimes we would even recruit friends to play postman for us.

One day, my friend's father accepted a job that meant their family would have to leave the country. I was very sad to think I would never be able to see her again, so we promised to keep sending each other letters. Going to the post office became a magical moment for me. She would send me candy and sweets from Brazil, many of which I had never tried, and I sent her things from Chile that she missed, accompanied by postcards I had made myself. What I liked best was waiting in line to post my parcel; I felt I was able to pack a small part of me to send to her. To this day we keep in touch.

Later, when I first moved to Barcelona to study, my mother would send me all the things I missed from Chile, as well as family photos to help me feel closer to home. It's very nice to open a package that contains not only the things that you are expecting or have asked for, but small surprises, too.

My life revolves around travel, and my embroidery classes have allowed me to visit many countries. I like collecting old threads and things that are related to embroidery, and I love to make small embroideries and send them to friends. I like to collect small treasures (as well as new friends) on every trip. I keep the treasures in a box until I feel the impulse to write; then, I let my intuition shape the package before I head to the post office.

When I travel to Japan, I buy things to send to friends in Spain and Chile, since many of them find it very difficult to travel. I share lots of pictures of my travels with them, too, so even though I travel alone, they always accompany me in a way.

Community

Giving back to a community member

letters from community members telling the recipient how much he or she means to them

homemade chocolate truffles (page 104), or wrap a high-quality fancy chocolate bar to match the package

homemade cookies (page 92)

cosy socks

bottle of wine or champagne (if appropriate)

herbal tea in handmade tea bags (page 82)

freshly ground coffee in a decorated bag

beautiful hardback book on a subject they love, signed by community members

fruit, vegetables and herbs grown in your garden

handmade journal (page 50)

USB of interesting podcasts to suit their job or hobbies

Charity packages

Always check with your local charity to see how best you can cater to their needs.

For children's charities

children's toys

backpacks

school supplies

new shoes

For animal shelters

clean second-hand blankets and towels

pet supply gift cards

cat and dog toys

pet shampoo

For families in need

tinned food – food you would want to eat (or which makes up part of a dish) is appreciated most

good-quality long-life pantry items

department store gift cards

For homeless charities

blankets

towels

toiletries

prepaid public transport tickets

For asylum seeker charities

good-quality long-life pantry items

department store gift cards

prepaid phone cards

welcome letters

present your offering simply

PDXCC Members: Nancy Wynne, David Pizzuti, Alayna Cato, Wesley Anne Cook, Lulieville, Miss Polly, Jillyn Chang, Philatelic Atrocities, Crisispanty, Parrot Post, IZ, Kearin, and Eva Moon Press
Portland, Oregon

letter-writing materials

PDXCC
PO BOX 26
Carlton North
Victoria 3054
Australia

wrapped with love and care

origami turtle to brighten the day

THE PORTLAND CORRESPONDENCE CO-OP

The Portland Correspondence Co-op (PDXCC) is a group of artists that gathers monthly around the motto of 'meet, make, mail'. Since attending the first meeting in January 2015, I have met many new friends in an increasing number of regular members each month. This simple motto has given me a new hobby and a way to connect with other creative people in Portland.

Our meetings consist of a formal presentation during the first hour, ranging from eclectic mail art demonstrations to the finer points of fountain pens. The second half of each meeting is a lively exchange of artist stamps made of paper or another medium stamped in each person's handmade PDXCC passport. Many stamps have a story behind them, or follow a theme of the artist's aesthetic.

Outside of the regular meetings, there is a monthly mail art swap. One person picks a theme and those who sign up make mail around that theme and send their creation to everyone on the list. It's a fun way to try new ideas and share creativity throughout the month. On months that I have participated in the swap, receiving so many beautiful postcards is such a delight and makes for many good mail days.

Sometimes there are events announced during meetings that keep us busy before the next gathering, such as a member's gallery show, stationery pop-up shop, or celebration of International Typewriter Day.

Occasionally, I also love to gather with PDXCC friends for a cup of tea and pastries at our favourite luncheonette.

I am thankful that PDXCC is open to anyone: there are people who attend just out of curiosity, and there are those who have been making mail art and corresponding with pen pals all over the world for many years. There is no 'look' that everyone is supposed to adhere to and the atmosphere is always light-hearted and welcoming.

We compiled a cheerful mail art parcel, including an honorary membership to the PDXCC, for a child staying at The Royal Children's Hospital in Melbourne.

Julia Neises

PDXCC meeting photography by Yves Johnson

What sponsoring children means to me

As soon as I finished university, months before I found a job, I decided to sponsor a child. I had been a little frustrated and stressed because I hadn't found the right job yet, but I caught an ad for Child Fund on television one night and immediately stopped feeling sorry for myself. I started to think about how trivial my first-world problems seemed compared to those experienced by people living in the third world. I remember thinking, I will get a job and will start making money soon, so I can finally do this!

My first sponsor child's name was Logos Agnes. Agnes is one of my favourite names and I was a logo designer for quite a while before I started designing books, so it felt like it was meant to be. Logos Agnes left her village in her early teens which meant Child Fund could no longer organise sponsorship for her. I currently sponsor Higenyi Hyubi. He is in grade five, doing well at school and was recently given a goat! He sends me lovely postcards from the Kadenge

Community in Uganda. If you have a sponsor child, would like to sponsor a child or want to send a care package to a sponsored community, I hope this care package provides for some inspiration. Anything you send will be welcomed. Your sponsor child or the community will not be receiving a lot of international mail. Make it personal, and decorate it with things from your family and home town.

Including a letter in your package is very important. Write a little about yourself: where you live, what you do for a job, what your hobbies are, and if you have any siblings, pets or children. Describe the country you come from: the landscape, the weather, the house you live in. Make sure your handwriting is legible, as your sponsor child has most likely just started learning English. Perhaps get other members of your family to write a little hello, too. If you have or know a child around the same age, encourage him or her to write a letter about your

city from a child's perspective; it could lead to the two children becoming pen friends!

Some items to include:

long-life biscuits or other non-perishable treats – something to share with family and friends

something a young person of the same age from your country would like – for example, a toy or game

a children's book written by a local author, especially one that shows what your culture is like

postcards or photographs of your town or city

photographs of you, your family and pets (see photo book, page 72)

a family scrapbook containing photos, newspaper clippings, drawings, stickers and more

something handmade – for example, a soft toy or socks

a map of the world highlighting where they are and where you are

cotton t-shirts a girl or boy of the same age would wear in your home town

pens and pencils and a handmade journal (see page 50)

I've redesigned the cover of one of my favourite books

Little Red Riding Hood loved care packages!

try using something recycled as the cover base and collage over the on top of it

homemade
mini pudding

handmade
Christmas
decorations

Orphan's Christmas

For someone far away

handmade card (see page 84) and newsy, cheery letter

items that remind your loved one of their family, friends and home

photo book (pages 72–75)

mini country flag

daggy local souvenir

favourite magazine

family/friendship group photograph

local sweet treats and snacks

Christmas crackers

handmade Christmas decoration

homemade fruitcake or Christmas cookies (taking weight into consideration)

mini Christmas stockings with individually wrapped items inside

For someone close by

handmade card (see page 84)

mini desk-sized Christmas tree

homemade fruitcake or Christmas cookies

cheese and fruit platter

Christmas crackers

handmade Christmas decoration

mulled wine spices

champagne, wine or homemade eggnog

think about the
sort of items you
would love if
you were feeling
isolated

ABCDEFGHIJK
Hello,
My name is
My Eve.
Welcome to
Australia.
I am 9
years old
and I like
to do gymnastics
and play piano
I hope you
enjoy life here.
LMNOPQRSTUV.

this parcel
includes maps,
reading cards,
sweets, soap and
a crafting kit

include letters
from children

handmade cat
soft toy is
holding a glow-
in-the-dark star

TRISHA GARNER AND RACHEL TERKELSEN

Graphic designers and asylum seeker advocates Melbourne, Australia

It's a small but important gesture: the act of sending a care package to an asylum seeker detained indefinitely on a remote, impoverished island, or to a refugee living in a desert camp, waiting to find a home. The injustices of war and inhumane government polices that terrorise the most vulnerable people on the planet can make you feel like howling at the moon in despair.

But bundling up a little package can carry a lot of emotional weight. A care package lets asylum seekers know that we care. It's an expression of kindness, compassion and connection. When you flee for your life, you lose your family and community and your sense of connection.

It's a challenge to work out what to include. What does one put into a package for a baby born in detention, who doesn't know how to smile? Or a forgotten child, robbed of their childhood?

Thoughtfulness is key. A handmade soft toy is a gift from the heart. A dictionary is both practical and empowering, together with notebooks and pens. Making a cloth cover adds a personal touch. Consider wrapping the parcel in a fun shape or keeping the wrapping transparent. That way it won't look like official correspondence from the government. There are great people in amazing not-for-profit organisations who visit detainees and refugees and understand the ins and outs, so consultation with an advocate is really helpful.

A friend who lives overseas looks up to the night sky when she's feeling homesick. Gazing at the moon and stars is a way of feeling connected to her mum. Seeing the same moon her mother can see. One big sky connecting the whole world.

A care package is like bundling up a hug that sends a message of love and humanity. A message of connection. Through the moon and the stars.

PO Box 26

While working on my book *Snail Mail* I opened a PO Box and invited my Instagram friends and followers to send me a decorated letter and be part of my book. I was so overwhelmed by the response; I was sent so many wonderful letters from all corners of the globe. For this book, I did a call-out for petite parcels and mini packages to be sent through the post or delivered to the post office. Again, the response was simply amazing. All of the packages are on the next few pages and the opened packages are dotted throughout the book. There are petite parcels from America, Argentina, Australia, Denmark, France, Japan, Malaysia, New Zealand, Sweden, Switzerland and the United Kingdom. Thank you, dear PO Box 26 petite parcel creators, for your amazing contributions. This book is so much richer with your artistry and personal stories.

Alice Oehr
Alison Ridgeway
Amanda Paino
Amy Devereux
Brigitte Forster
Catherine Insch
Cassandre, Palavas Paris
Catherine Gemanel
Chanie, Dave, Ponie, Nancy and Honey
Emma Jay
Emma van Leest
Ethel Manibo
Fiona Ling
Hannah Bougouizi
Hannah Gumbo
Heather Menzies

Helen, Happymail_
Katrina Alana
Kylie Mahar
Ingrid Josephine
Keiko Vogel
Puk Hyllested Hansen
Jane and Marcus
Jane Ormond
Jane Wallace Mitchell
Jenn Heui
Jenna Templeton
Jess Racklyeft
Jessica McLean
Joanna, Kikuhouse
Jude McIntyre
Justine Betts
Kumiko Tasaki
Lina Gonzalez

Louise, The Design Find
Lydia, Peace Love and Pom Poms
Makiko Sugita
Mandy Gaultier
Marce, yosoymars
Mary Boukouvalas
Mahshed Hooshmand
May, Olivia, Joel and Sylvie
Meaghan Green
Melanie Klassen
Monika Huber
Natalie Kotitsas
Natasha Zangmeister
Niina Aoki
Nina Larkins
Paige Harrington

Pacquita Maher
Kate Holderness
Katie-Jane MacConnachie
Raquel Téllez-Wiklund
Rose De Angelis
Sharon Brookes
Sheree Coleman
Sheridan Forde
Simone Hart
Stephanie and Frida
Susan Fitzgerald
Tara Watts
Tarryn Carr
Thomas Vogel, Tozai Design
Tina Thompson
Trish, Hobby Hoppers

Trish sent me this wonderful parcel, but, unfortunately, it is missing in action. It is such a shame when the post lets you down! I am so happy she took a photo of it so we can all enjoy it, even if it's lost on its travels. I hope someone is enjoying it somewhere.

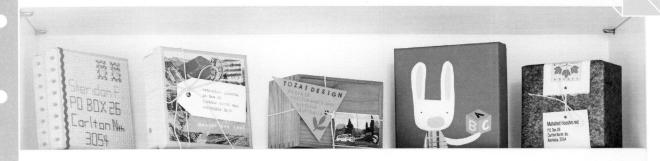

THIS WAY UP

Templates

BLOW UP BY 140%, SO YOUR SQUARE MEASURES 210 MM X 210 MM (8¼ IN X 8¼ IN)

ORIGAMI PHOTO BOOK

BLOW UP BY 140%, SO YOUR SQUARE MEASURES 100 MM X 100 MM (4 IN X 4 IN)

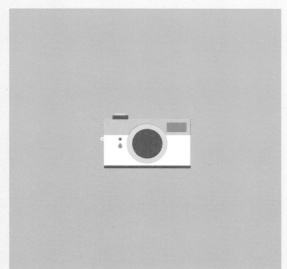

NAIVE HAND-STITCHING

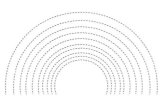

MAKE AT ANY SIZE YOU LIKE

MINI CONGRATS FLAG

MAKE AT ANY SIZE YOU LIKE

EXAMPLE ON PAGE 176

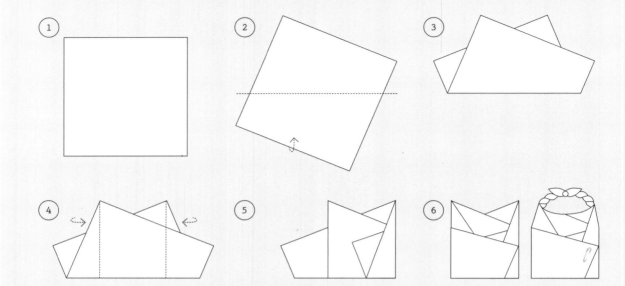

① ② ③

④ ⑤ ⑥

EXAMPLE ON PAGE 183

① ② ③

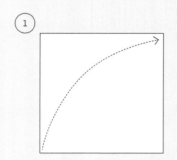
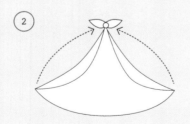

EXAMPLE ON PAGE 119

TO PLACE ON COFFEE BAGS 98 MM (3¾ IN) IN WIDTH BLOW UP BY 275%

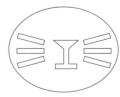

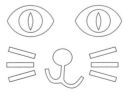

BLOW UP BY 170%, SO YOUR CD COVER IS A4, 210 MM X 297 MM (8¼ IN X 11¼ IN)

USE AT ANY SIZE YOU LIKE!

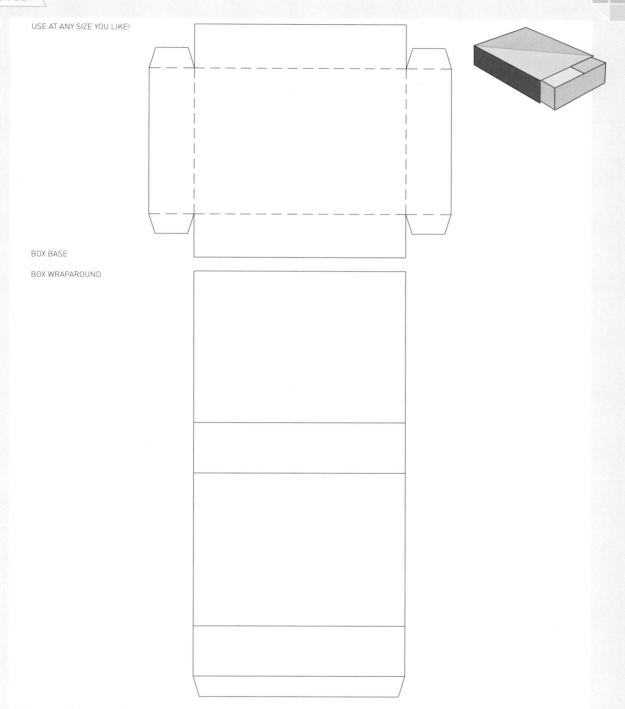

BOX BASE

BOX WRAPAROUND

USE AT ANY SIZE YOU LIKE!

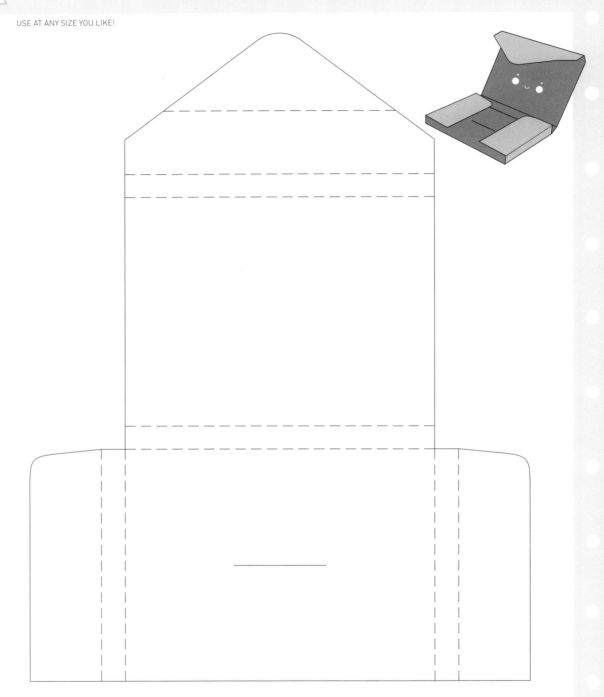

USE AT ANY SIZE YOU LIKE!

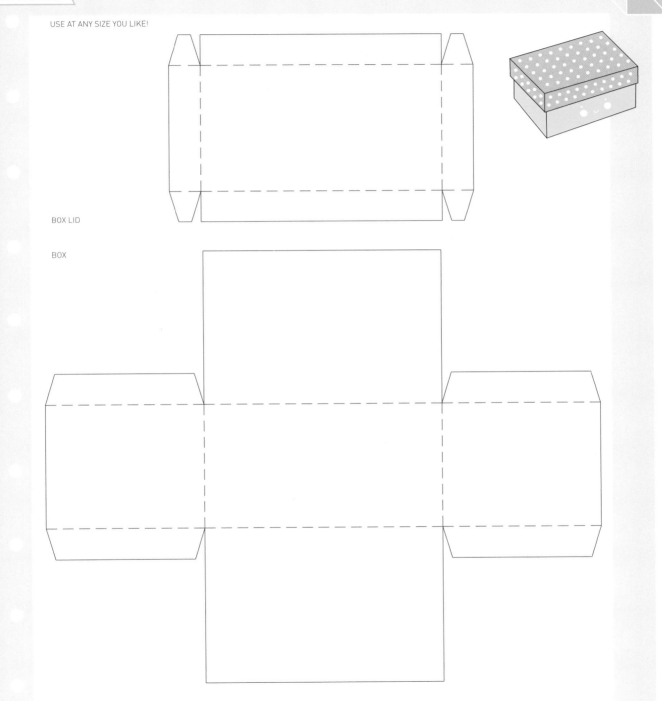

BOX LID

BOX

USE AT ANY SIZE YOU LIKE!

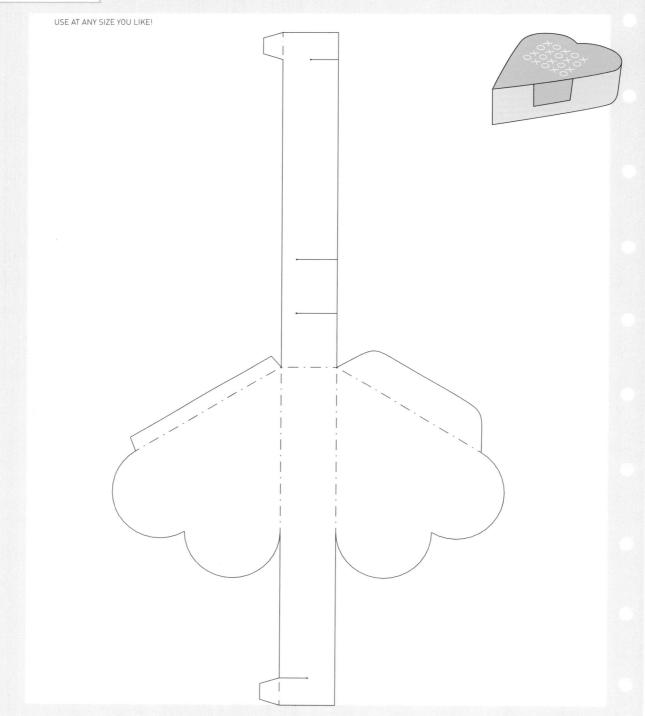

USE AT ANY SIZE YOU LIKE!

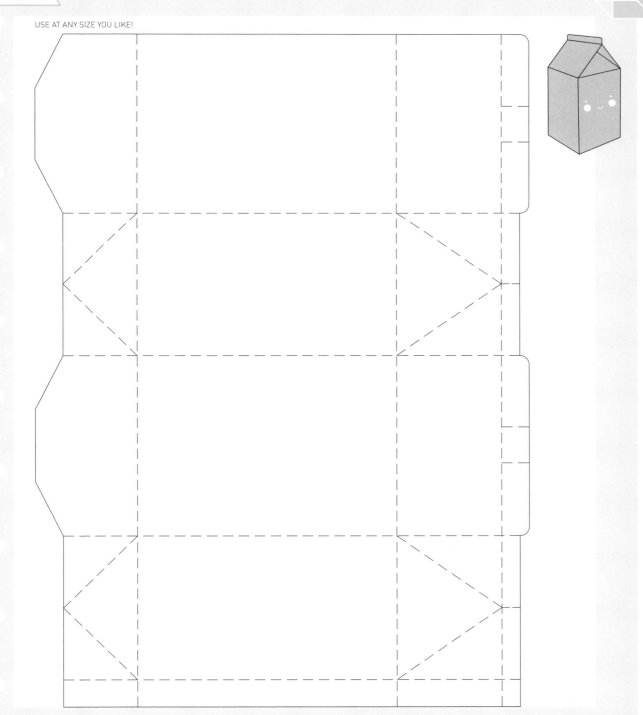

Thank you so much to my publisher, Jane Willson, and to Julie Pinkham. Your ongoing support and faith in me means the world to me. Thank you so much for helping me make this book with all of the support I needed. I think it shows on the pages how much I have been looked after and cared for as an author.

Thank you to my most wonderful editor, Rihana Ries. This book would not exist without your expertise, guidance and wonderful ideas. I absolutely love working with you and hope we make many more beautiful books together in the future.

Thank you to Mr Mark Campbell. Your design eye on the photoshoots, support and style advice are crucial to this book.

Thank you to Paul McNally and Lucy Heaver, for all the wonderful work you have done in helping me realise my lifelong dream to be an author.

Thank you to Chris Middleton: you always go above and beyond. Your lighting and eye for detail have produced the most beautiful photographs for this book.

Thank you to Todd Rechner, for your production expertise and for always making sure we have the very best and most beautiful colours and binding.

Thank you in advance to the wonderful HG PR team of Kasi, Erica and Roxy. You always help me feel comfortable in the most nerve-wracking situations and always do that little bit extra.

Thank you to Alice Oehr, for your outstanding modelling, for bringing a wonderful lunch to the shoot and for all your support and friendship.

Thank you to May Yeung and Sylvie Yeung-Boschler for all of Sylvie's wonderful modelling on the pages of this book, for May's amazing ability to keep Miss S interested and engaged, and for bringing us all coffee and food. Thank you to Olivia Yeung and Joel Silver for making the most delicious congee and dropping it over after the shoot so we had something warm and nourishing for dinner.

Thank you to Steve Wide, for all of your support, love and ideas, not just for the making of this book, but for each and every day of our lives.

Thank you to all of the guest package and story contributors. Thank you for enriching this book with your heartfelt words, beautiful work and passion. Each one of you has added such a special piece to these pages. Thank you to Beci Orpin, Flora Waycott, Heather Menzies, Hiki Komura, Jane Ormond, The Ulman/Eisner family (Kate, Bren, Vivienne, Indi, Jazzy and Pepper), Keiko Vogel and Noah Kristensen, Laura Ameba, Magdalena Franco, Margaret Haas, The BS Club (Adeline, Alice, Beci and Steve), The Portland Correspondence Co-Op and Julia Neises, and Trisha Garner and Rachel Terkelsen.

Thank you to Emma Jay, for lending me your wonderful vintage cameras and divine pink mug.

Thank you to Hiki for taking time out of your busy schedule to be in my Tokyo photoshoot!

Thank you to my family: Mum, Andrew, Dee, Olive and Leo, Carolyn, Evie and Velvet, Paul and Steve.

Thank you to my wonderful friends: Melinda, Audrey and Hugo, Pacquita, Mark and Will, May and Sylvie, Olivia and Joel, Jane and Will, Dawn and Steve, Ingrid and Adrian, Beci and Alice, Hiki and Ryo, Kate B, Graham, Trisha, Rache, Tam, Marianna, Mandy, Kate U, Pip and Makiko.

Thank you to the wonderful PO Box 26 petite parcel-makers and the incredible community on Instagram. And a BIG thank-you to Emma and Ethel, who created such beauty whilst battling serious illnesses.

Thank you to everyone who has made me a care package: the Wide family in Australia, after my accident, and Colin and Muriel Wide in the UK; when Steve and I had not two pennies to rub together, you sent us onto a train ride to Scotland with freshly baked bread, homemade jam and the best butter I have ever eaten, fresh from the local farm. Your kindness and generosity will never be forgotten. And to Chris and Katrine for taking us birdwatching, and showing us hedgehogs, the ultimate travel care package!

Published in 2016 by Hardie Grant Books

Hardie Grant Books (Australia)
Ground Floor, Building 1
658 Church Street
Richmond, Victoria 3121
www.hardiegrant.com.au

Hardie Grant Books (UK)
5th & 6th Floors
52–54 Southwark Street
London SE1 1UN
www.hardiegrant.co.uk

A Cataloguing-in-Publication entry is available from the catalogue of the National Library of Australia at www.nla.gov.au

Care Packages

ISBN 9781743791387

Publisher/Publishing Director: Lucy Heaver and Jane Willson
Editor: Rihana Ries
Design Manager: Mark Campbell
Designer, art director and illustrator: Michelle Mackintosh
Photographer: Chris Middleton
Production Manager: Todd Rechner

Colour reproduction by Splitting Image Colour Studio

Printed and bound in China by 1010 Printing International Limited

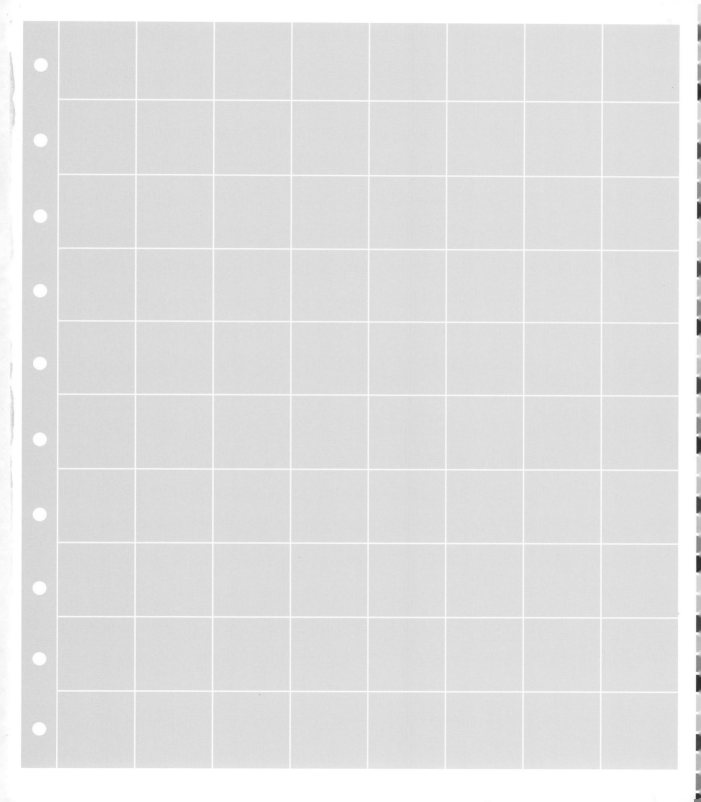

THIS WAY UP